simply pillows

Sunset
simply
pillows

BY THE EDITORS OF SUNSET BOOKS

SUNSET BOOKS INC. • MENLO PARK, CA

SUNSET BOOKS INC.

Director, Sales & Marketing: Richard A. Smeby

Editorial Director: Bob Doyle

Production Director: Lory Day

Art Director: Vasken Guiragossian

SIMPLY PILLOWS was produced in conjunction with
Roundtable Press, Inc.

Directors: Marsha Melnick, Susan E. Meyer

STAFF FOR THIS BOOK:

Developmental Editor: Linda J. Selden

Senior Editor: Carol Spier

Book Design: Areta Buk/Thumb Print

Sample Coordinator and Technical Advisor: Linda Lee/Linda Lee Design Associates

Illustrations: Celia M. Mitchell

Photo Research: Ede Rothaus

Editorial Assistant: John Glenn

Production Coordinator: Patricia S. Williams

Cover Photograph: Philip Harvey; *Photo Direction:* JoAnn Masaoka Van Atta

Photography acknowledgments appear on page 128.

ISBN 0-376-01433-4

Library of Congress Catalog Card Number: 97-60841

Printed in the United States

For additional copies of SIMPLY PILLOWS or any other *Sunset* book,
call 1-800-526-5111.

foreword

when you add a pillow to a chair, sofa, or bed you enhance the
furniture by making it more inviting and finishing its design. Whatever your
reason for adding pillows to your decor—to add color, pattern, embellishment,
elegance, interest, or comfort—you'll find that making a pillow is a two-part
process—design decisions first, sewing second.

Simply Pillows is an inspirational and practical guide to pillow making. It's
filled with design ideas, includes more than thirty projects with step-by-step
directions, and has a concise guide to the basic techniques you'll use.

Part One: Be Creative encourages you to put on your design cap and think
creatively. It helps you to analyze the way pillows will be used in your decor,
to make informed design choices, and to select suitable materials. Photos of
pillows in different styles and settings allow you to visualize the possibilities,
whereas the text gives an overview of the design process. This section will
help you to choose pillows you can make and use with pleasure.

Part Two: Projects features a selection of great-looking pillows and detailed,
illustrated directions for making them. The designs range from tailored to
elegant, from casual to sweet to sophisticated, and
are grouped by basic method of construction. Most
projects are simple and can be made quickly even if
you have little sewing experience; a few owe their
charm to their intricate details.

As you look at the projects, you'll begin to see
that many of them are based upon ideas that can
easily be transferred to pillows of other shapes and
sizes. Several of the projects include a special
Designer Detail. These are construction and trimming
techniques that add distinction; they're written
generically so you can easily adapt them to other
situations.

Part Three: Basics covers the general planning,
cutting, and sewing techniques you'll use. It also
explains the equipment you should have on hand.

Whether you make one of the featured projects or
design your own pillow, we encourage you to adapt
the ideas and directions to suit your decor and taste.
Mix and match shapes and details; change color,
fabric, and trim—be creative.

table of **contents**

part three
basics 106

designer details

be creative

PILLOWS ARE SIMPLY WONDERFUL DECORATIVE accessories. Place one on a piece of furniture and you'll instantly add style, color, and comfort. Add an array to a sofa or window seat, and you'll transform its look. Change pillows with the seasons, and your decor can reflect the shift in light and air. There are few accessories that offer such versatility—pillows can emphasize, refine, contrast, complement, or mask the furniture they sit upon, dressing it up or down, unifying disparate pieces in a room, or drawing the eye to a place of special merit. Think plain, think fancy, think of fabrics homespun or luxurious, of trims humble or ornate—be imaginative, be inspired, you'll find it impossible to make only one pillow.

thinking creatively

the possibilities for pillow designs are virtually limitless. Perhaps the most challenging aspect of the design process lies in setting some parameters so you can narrow your choices. You are probably planning to make a pillow for a specific location—a chair, sofa, bench, window seat, or bed. Luckily, this purpose will give your creative thinking a head start. To begin, analyze this location and determine what shape, style, and fabrication of pillow will best suit your needs.

What are the characteristics of the furniture? Is it hard or soft? Is it colorful? Patterned? Plain? Does it have an inherent design or period style that you want to complement? Is it formal or informal? How much use does it get? How many pillows will you want on it? Does it matter what shape they are? Should the pillows be firm, moderately soft, or really squishy?

What about pillow shape? Square? Rectangular? Round? Cylindrical? Some other geometric or free-form shape? Do you want a bolster that sits firmly against the arm or back of a sofa or daybed?

How will the pillow be used? Tossed among other throw pillows or against bed pillows? Leaned against sofa cushions? Are you trying to soften hard furniture? Do you need a cushion you can sit on rather than a throw pillow? Will the pillow be used indoors or out?

ABOVE: This lively assortment of plaids and prints would make a lovely group of pillows. A shared palette and variety of scales unify the mix; the moiré prints add a soft touch.
BELOW: Lush floral fabric needs no special embellishment to hold its own on wicker porch furniture. These cushions use basic knife-edge and boxed constructions.

What about style and fabrication? Should the pillow be tailored? Formal? Traditional? Eclectic? Casual? Do you want it to coordinate with other items in your decor? Is it one of a set? Will you be using elegant or luxurious fabrics and trims or simple ones? Do you plan to combine several fabrics on one pillow or keep the fabrication plain? Are you thinking of ruffles? Fringe? Tassels? Buttons?

How much money are you willing to spend? Most pillows are not very large and don't require a lot of fabric or trim, which is precisely the reason you should answer this question! It's easy to fall in love with wonderful materials when you won't need much of them, but don't be surprised when you start to add up the bill. However, if you compare the cost of materials to the cost of purchasing pillows from a good furnishings vendor, you'll see that making your own is likely to be much more economical.

Once you have a general idea of the type of pillow you'd like to have, you can really plunge into the creative part of the design process and choose the details and fabrics that make a pillow special. As you plan your project, consider not only the answers to the preceding questions but also your experience with sewing. Most pillows are simple and fairly quick to make, but the more comfortable you are using a sewing machine and the better equipped your work space, the easier you'll find the process. And always bear in mind that any pillow can be made in almost any size—the construction methods are not dependent upon the size of the pieces.

This red and ecru bedroom ensemble is so thoughtfully designed it's not until you take a second look that you realize six fabrics were used. From back to front, note the graduated pillow sizes, crisp knife-pleated tattersall ruffles, striped bias welting between the complementary red ruffle and the pillow body (they're on the hanging also), luxurious fringe at the ends of the damask pillows, and deep frills on the neckroll pillow.

pillow design

Fabrics with woven-in patterns add textural as well as graphic interest. Most of this tailored assortment is fairly dressy, but common colors make the sportier green twill and coarser ikat check good additions, The glazed surface of the cherry-color chintz adds a nice counterpoint.

Pale sculptural shells can be an interesting alternative to buttons. They're important yet understated against the plain lines of these linen shams.

as you look through this book, you'll see that most pillow designs are just variations on one of three basic pillow types—knife-edge, square-edge, and cylindrical. It's the details of the variations and the way in which fabric and trim are used that make the pillows special. While you are planning your project, remember that you don't need a complicated design to make a great-looking pillow. A basic design, well made in a plain fabric, will have an understated elegance—and you needn't add anything to a spectacular fabric to turn it into a spectacular pillow. On the other hand, there are so many ways to manipulate and embellish fabric, such a wealth of ribbons, fringes, tassels, cording, and such lovely buttons, that it's sometimes difficult to resist the possibilities—and if they appeal, why should you?

Just as any pillow can be made in nearly any size, so can it be made in nearly any fabrication. In fact, your choice of fabric and trim can completely transform the character of the design. For instance, a basic knife-edge pillow—two identical pieces of fabric sewn togther around the perimeter and stuffed—can be understated in plain linen or cotton, more important in chenille or velvet, cute in calico, sporty in a country-style plaid or check, exotic in a batik, or elegant in a beautiful silk damask. Add welting to the perimeter of each interpretation and the effect will be tailored. Add tassel fringe and, depending upon the fabric and fringe type, it will be either fun or more elegant. Add a ruffle and it will be sweet or fancy. And this is just a beginning!

Inspiration for pillow designs is everywhere. Armchair research is easy— almost any magazine you open is likely to have photos of people sitting on furniture with pillows, and, of course, many publications are devoted to interior design. If you have access to an international magazine vendor, take advantage of the European design magazines—you don't have to be able to read them to appreciate their style. Travel magazines provide inspiration for eclectic and unusual fabrications. Home furnishings catalogs are another good source for ideas. Clip photos of any pillows that appeal to you and also of interesting fabric or color combinations that might work with your decor. For a hands-on look at design possibilities go shopping. Visit home furnishings stores to see how pillows are used, how they can be embellished, how fabrics are mixed and manipulated. If you've sewn a lot of clothing,

think of all the dressmaker details you can borrow—embellishments you might consider too contrived or costumey for your wardrobe can sometimes make a superb addition to your decor.

You can also take your design inspiration directly from the materials. If your pillows are to coordinate with existing furnishings, you may already have fabrics on hand. If you sew a lot, you may have leftover yardage or large scraps. Perhaps you do needlework—needlepoint, cross-stitch, crewel, and patchwork are all terrific candidates for pillow tops. Perhaps you're a textile lover who simply can't resist collecting unusual fabrics, trims, buttons, and beads from flea markets, antique stores, or vacation travels. Let any of these materials spark a design idea. Analyze them and pick out their special features: a prominent motif that can be centered, a figured stripe that might make a great mitered border, a scalloped edge that would make an interesting ruffle, a sheer that would be intriguing as an overlay, a changeable silk that will shimmer when gathered. The wonderful thing about pillows is that you can combine materials to create great effects, so even if you've only a small amount of something you can probably use it to advantage.

If your decorating plans call for a group of pillows, you can make multiples of one design, make coordinating variations, or make an eclectic mix. For instance, when making multiples of one design, choose several complementary fabrics and place them differently on each pillow. Or make identical pillows in several sizes. Or focus several designs around one print or plaid, trimming

Bold graphic pillows are a fitting complement to the offbeat color scheme of this bedroom. Note how the pillow designs are really very simple, it's the shapes and colors that provide the impact.

pillow design

each with a second fabric or a complementary trim. Or let color be the unifying force, using assorted fabrics or diverse pillow shapes, but making all the same hue. Or choose one fabric type—chenille, canvas, linen—and use an array of solid colors. Take your color or materials cue from the rest of your decor and let the pillow fabrication be as straightforward or full of surprises as you wish.

Pleasing proportions are as important to pillow design as the fabric and trim. Because pillows are three dimensional, it can be difficult to imagine how large they should be. Don't hesitate to mock up a pillow and test it on your furniture before actually making it. You can fold, stack, or roll towels to get an idea of the proper size. If your fabric has a motif or stripe that you wish to feature, wrap or lay it over the mock-up to be sure you'll be using it to best advantage; you might discover that the pillow size should be adjusted. If you are considering a ruffle, mock up a section from a fabric scrap or paper to see how deep it should be. If your pillow coordinates with other furnishings, you might want to match some element of their proportions—for instance, a pillow ruffle might be half the depth of a slipcover skirt or the width of a band of trim might be the same as a matching band on the draperies.

While you are planning your design, give some thought to the way the pillow will be filled. The firmer the inner pillow form, the stiffer and larger it will look. Firm throw pillows actually take up more space than soft ones because they don't respond to pressure when they're leaned against—a firm pillow that is too large can make its chair less rather than more comfortable. If you'd like to be able to sink into your pillow or want it to look relaxed rather than perky, fill it with down and/or feathers. Ready-made foam, polyester-, and down-filled pillow forms are widely available in sewing and home furnishings stores and catalogs, and you can easily cut them down to create the size you need. More information about pillow forms can be found in Part Three, Basics.

TOP: Fabrics with a common regional heritage, such as these French country prints, are easy companions.
BOTTOM: When mixing prints with stripes, you'll find it easier to make selections if you pick a theme, such as these garden images.
RIGHT: Use a fabric picture to turn a pillow into a conversation piece. Sew panels to opposite sides of a pillow; knot them at the center; secure the ends with rubber bands.

choosing fabric

the fabric makes the pillow. Although shape and construction are certainly important, it's the fabric that provides real character. Happily, you can use almost any fabric to make pillows. There are many kinds of fabric; if you understand their qualities, you'll be able to choose the ones that will work best for the project you have in mind.

When you are designing it is important to think about the aesthetic as well as the practical characteristics of fabric. Fabric allows you to introduce color, pattern, and texture to your decor. *Pattern* may relate to or establish a style. When you think of styles such as country, lodge, French or English, Victorian or other periods, distinct pattern images come to mind for each. *Color* establishes mood and can change your perception of space or proportion—and some palettes are associated with specific decorating styles. *Texture* contributes to the way fabric reflects or absorbs light, and thus affects its color. Fabrics can have a smooth, soft, crisp, or coarse texture—or a combination of these. Fabrics such as bouclé, velvet, and matelassé have texture that adds dimension. The structure of a fabric's weave, the type and weight of the fiber it is made from, and the finish it is given all contribute to its texture. These last characteristics also give each kind of fabric its *hand*—a term used to describe the way a fabric handles or behaves, indicating how stable it is and how well it will mold over a pillow form or gather into a ruffle.

Confused? Even though you may not be familiar with the jargon applied to fabrics, you should use your eyes and hands to get an idea of the effect a fabric is likely to have when made into a specific pillow design. Visit furniture stores to get a firsthand look at the way different fabrics are used, and try to handle a good-sized sample of any fabric you contemplate using before you purchase it. If possible, look at samples in the room and on the furniture where the pillow will be used to be sure you like the effect.

A boxed seat cushion and big knife-edge pillows make this iron chair as comfortable as an upholstered piece. The plain plaid sham is charming with the button closure turned to the front.

choosing fabric

ABOVE: Base a pillow group around one fabric, such as velvet, in a variety of hues, and supplement with a few complementary textures—here some silk shantung, a damask, and a tapestry.

BELOW: Rug fragments make attractive pillows. Pick a style that suits your decor, and center the patterns or not, as the fragments permit.

What kind of fabric should you use? In general, home furnishings fabrics—often called *decorator fabrics*—are best. They not only offer great aesthetic options with coordinated lines of different scale patterns, diverse wovens, and good solids, but they've also been engineered to have a suitable hand, to wear well, and often to be stain resistent. Additionally, they're usually quite wide (54"–60") so they may be more efficient to work with. Depending upon where you live, a wide selection of decorator fabrics may be available at local fabric stores. If not, you can often order them through a furnishings store or interior designer. Consider also fabrics designed for quilt making—they offer many of the aesthetic advantages of decorator fabrics, but are usually only 45" wide.

Apparel fabrics can also be used very effectively for pillows. Just give some thought to the way you'll be handling a fabric to be sure it will hold up, and, if appropriate, back it with an interfacing or lining fabric to give it more body. In fact, clever use of apparel fabrics can result in some unexpected and sophisticated pillow fabrications. Consider using soft velvet to create a graceful flange or doubled organza to make a perky but sheer ruffle; experiment with layering sheers over prints or brocades; or use exotic eveningwear fabrics such as crystal-pleated metallics to make the simplest but most elegant throw pillows.

When you are considering fabrics, don't confuse fiber with fabric. Fiber is what fabric is made of. Fibers are either natural—cotton, linen, silk, wool—or man-made. Some man-made fibers are created from natural materials: rayon, for example, is derived from wood. Others, such as nylon, polyester, and acrylic, are true synthetics; these are often petroleum-based. The way a fiber is spun, woven, and finished determines the kind of fabric it becomes. There are a great many kinds of fabric (broadcloth, velveteen, chintz, damask—to name just a few), and many, but not all, can be made from more than one fiber.

Decorator fabrics are often blends of cotton and other fibers, usually linen or rayon, but sometimes silk or wool or a synthetic such as polyester. Elegant fabrics sometimes feature metallic threads as well. Linen, rayon, and silk all add sheen and take dye well, so fabrics made with them often appear luxurious and have especially intense colors. Cotton and wool are both durable. Cotton decorator fabrics come in many weaves, weights, and finishes, and are easy to handle. Like cotton, silk comes in many textures, weights, and finishes, and the different silks have widely varying characteristics—ranging from fragile to durable, easy to handle to frustratingly slippery. Some silks water-spot easily and a single drop of condensation from a cold glass can make them look soiled. Most silks are extremely sensitive to sunlight; they fade badly and sometimes deteriorate with constant exposure. Fabrics with a high synthetic content sometimes pucker, melt under the iron, or hold stains, but they can also have interesting qualities, so experiment with any you find appealing.

Which fabric will be suitable? For a pillow, just about anything goes, so you can base your selection on what will look best on the furniture, make up to give the desired effect, and hold up under the anticipated wear. The most important thing is that you take the time to think through how a specific fabric will work in a particular design. If you plan to work with unconventional materials, be sure you have the sewing equipment (or patience) to handle them. And if it's important that the pillow cover be washable, choose appropriate fabrics.

Medium-weight, nonpile, nonslippery fabrics with a stable weave are the easiest to work with. Some home furnishings fabrics have a glazed finish—cotton chintz being an example—some are treated with a stain repellent, and some are backed for durability; these finishes sometimes make the fabric less pliable. Fabrics that wrinkle easily will continue to wrinkle as pillows, which may or may not bother you. Loose, open weaves might need a lining so they won't reveal the inner pillow form. Velvets and heavy Jacquard or tapestry weaves, which can be awkward to use for larger sewing projects, are generally fine choices for pillows, which have fewer seams. Don't rule out nontraditional sewing materials—leathers, real and synthetic suedes, rug fragments, even some knits can all be effectively used to cover pillows. If you'll be combining fabrics, try to use pieces with similar qualities so the seams will be smooth and the weight even; or use unlike materials intentionally to create special effects.

Quilt blocks are always interesting as pillow tops. They're very much at home in a homespun setting such as this, but because they are naturally so graphic, they can be striking in contemporary settings. Use old quilt fragments or new blocks and have fun with the colors.

choosing trim

A monochrome color scheme becomes more interesting when texture is given a role. Punctuate a grouping of velvet, damask, and raw silk pillows with sheer ruffles or lighter weight welting or binding.

Use companion prints to tie together accessories and primary furnishings. These prints come from a manufacturer who makes both bedding and yard goods, but you can also use sheets as fabric. Note the simple welting that dresses up these pillows and the big bow that finishes the bolster.

buttons, welting, decorative cording, tassels, fringe, frogs, lace, ribbon, even sporty rickrack—trims add character to pillows. Generally, trims should be in scale with the pillow and have the same visual weight as the fabric; however, there are times when larger or heavier trims are very effective. Whether a trim should match or contrast the fabrics is a matter of taste and the effect desired.

Almost any pillow design will benefit from the addition of some trim, and many designs depend upon embellishment. A plain white linen or cotton sham will be much more interesting with a self-welting, a subtle band of white grosgrain ribbon, or an overlay of simple white lace. Perimeter seams and the inside edges of button bands are obvious places to embellish, but you can add trim to any seam, apply it to frame or dissect a pillow top where there are no seams, or stitch it along the edge of an applied band or a tuck, flange, or ruffle. You may want buttons to tuft a pillow or to secure a closure; there are thousands of styles to choose among or you can cover your own. Welting (fabric-covered cording) can be made from your fabric or one that complements it. Although apparel fabric stores often carry a variety of ribbon and lace, you'll probably find the best selection of trims in a home furnishings fabric store.

It you like trims, you're likely to find shopping for them both exhilarating and frustrating. There are so many choices, you'll no doubt be inspired to take advantage of them. But select wisely—you may be surprised by their cost. If trim is an important part of your pillow design, be sure you find what you want before you purchase the fabric; you may want to adjust one or the other until you find a mix that looks great and fits your budget.

Most decorator trims are made of cotton or rayon or a blend of the two. They come in myriad colors, yet finding a perfect match for your fabric may prove virtually impossible. But a trim that makes a subtle or strong contrast can be more interesting than one that blends into its background—that's why you use trim anyway. When you want a perfect match, welting may be the most appropriate choice. Some vendors can arrange to have such trims as tassels made to order and many good notions retailers have a button-covering service. If you plan to wash your pillow cover, be sure the trim is washable, and preshrink it before using.

into the **workroom**

gather your inspirational clippings, your fabrics and trims, and get ready to make some final decisions about your pillow. Whether you are making one of the projects from this book or one of your own design, you can get a good feeling for the effect of the finished pillow by looking at the materials. So it's wise to lay out the fabrics and trims in a rough approximation of your design and take a look at them. Are you happy with the relative proportions and the mix of colors and textures? If not, adjust or supplement them before you start cutting or sewing. Think through the assembly process to be sure you understand it; if you're working with materials different from those suggested, you may want to adapt the directions; or if you're making multiples of one design, you might see ways to work more efficiently.

Be creative, be focused, and if you are an inexperienced sewer, be confident. Most pillows are fun and not complicated to make, so be inspired—there's no reason not to make all your great ideas.

Small lace-covered satin pillows with eyelet ruffles are always romantic. These are carefully composed, with ribbons in lace beading placed over the background lace and finished with dainty bows.

part two

projects

IT'S A RARE DECORATING SCHEME THAT WON'T BE enhanced by a pillow. Following are more than thirty designs—tailored, casual, formal, elegant, witty—with directions. You can make them as shown or adapt them as suits your needs or fancy. Choose fabrics and trim that complement your decor, make the pillows in sizes appropriate to your furniture, or use your creativity to mix and match our ideas to create new designs. To smooth your work we've included many Tips from the Pros— helpful hints and tricks—throughout the directions. So browse through the photos to pick a design, read the step-by-step directions, refer to the watercolor illustrations, and get started.

how to use the directions

Each project in this book can be made by following its illustrated step-by-step directions. To understand the components of these directions, read these two pages.

1 A colored fabric panel begins each project. It contains information you need before you begin to sew.

2 ABOUT THE SAMPLE

Here you will find a description of the sample, including the fabric and trim, the finished dimensions, and any special design or construction features.

3 MATERIALS

A list of all materials needed, including notions and pillow forms.

✄ To calculate the amount of fabric or trim you need, you must measure the pillow form; refer to the cutting directions further down in the panel, the schematic drawings, and the step-by-step directions.

4 TECHNIQUES

This paragaph refers you to general construction information for the type of pillow featured and also to Part Three of the book, Basics, where you will find information to help you measure, calculate yardage, and sew. Review these sections, as they support and enhance the project directions. Use the index at the end of the book to locate specific information.

5 MEASURE, MARK, AND CUT

The note that begins this section alerts you to aspects of the project that may not be apparent from the photo, such as when to allow extra fabric for an overlap closure or pleats, where to add special seam allowance, or how to plan a ruffle. For instance, the note in this example tells you how to calculate the dimensions of the mitered bands.

6 CUTTING LIST

This names each piece needed to make the pillow, including facings and bias strips for welting, and tells you how many of each to cut.

✄ The letter identifying each piece is repeated in the schematic diagram and directions.

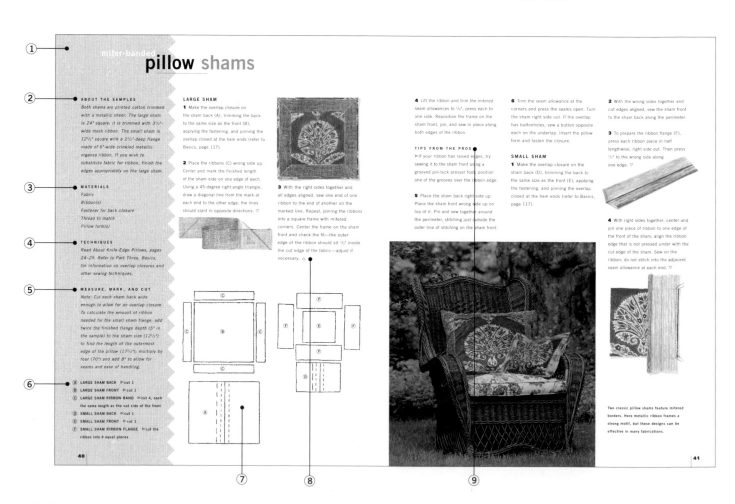

7 SCHEMATIC DIAGRAM(S)

Each project is accompanied by a drawing of its component pieces. These diagrams show the relative proportions of the pieces. Where pertinent, they are configured to show the relative positions of the pieces as well. For instance, on this example the ribbon bands that will be mitered to frame the pillows are arranged around each pillow front.

✄ The letter on each section identifies the piece as given in the cutting list. If there are multiples of small pieces, such as ties, one letter may label all.

✄ The solid lines on the schematics indicate cutting lines, usually at the perimeter of a piece.

✄ The short dash lines indicate foldlines, usually for hems.

✄ The long dash lines indicate an overlap alignment, usually for a closure.

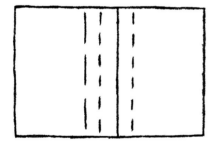

✄ If a component piece would be too long to fit proportionally on the schematic, it is broken by a small gap with two squiggle lines to indicate that a portion has been omitted; this most often occurs on pieces such as bias strips used for welting, or for ruffles. Cut and join these pieces as necessary.

✄ If the front and back of the project are identical, they may be drawn only once on the schematic; be sure to check the cutting list to see how many of each piece to cut.

✄ The schematic diagrams appear next to or within the colored fabric panel.

The schematic diagrams are *not* cutting layouts. Use them as a quick reference to identify and assemble the pieces. They'll also help you visualize the project if you wish to change it in some way. Refer to Part Three, Basics, to see how to make a cutting layout.

In a few of the projects, the schematic diagrams are accompanied by a **MEASURING DIAGRAM.** These clarify how to measure a pillow form or piece of furniture. Use them in conjunction with the note under Measure, Mark, and Cut, taking the measurements where indicated by the arrows.

8 STEP-BY-STEP DIRECTIONS

To make it easy to keep your place, each step of the directions is numbered. Review the information in the colored fabric panel, cut out your pillow pieces, and then follow the directions in the sequence given. Read the directions through before beginning, to be sure you understand the nature of the project.

✄ The first time a piece is handled, it is identified by letter as well as by name.

✄ If a step is illustrated, an arrow at the end of the step points to the pertinent illustration. The illustration can be above, below, or next to the text.

✄ If a technique or process is more fully explained in Part Three, this information is cross-referenced within the numbered steps.

9 TIPS FROM THE PROS

Throughout the project directions, we've included hints, tips, and words of wisdom to smooth your work. These usually follow the step to which they pertain, so read the step and the subsequent tips before proceeding.

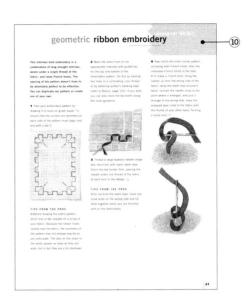

10 DESIGNER DETAIL

Several of the projects in this book are enhanced by special "designer details." Each has been placed under a colored fabric flag and explained with extra attention to ensure that you'll be able to sew it successfully.

✄ The use of these details is by no means limited to the ways in which we've featured them. The flags make it easy for you to see the details separately from the projects, and we encourage you to think of other ways to use them—so be creative.

THREE IMPORTANT NOTES

✄ The standard seam allowance for pillow making is $1/2$".

✄ Most of the directions assume you begin with a pillow form. In Part Three, Basics, you'll find information on purchasing, altering, and making forms.

✄ Any measurements given in the measuring note, cutting list, or step-by-step directions reflect those used to make the sample in the photo. Check and adjust the proportions to suit your needs.

about knife-edge pillows

In its simplest form, a knife-edge pillow is nothing more than two identical pieces of fabric sewn together around the edges and stuffed. A tailored sham—a cover with a central pocket that holds the form and an extending unstuffed border, or flange, all around—is an easy and good-looking variation on a basic knife-edge pillow. For either type, if you begin with a wonderful piece of fabric, cut the pillow so it shows off the pattern, and sew neatly, you really don't need to do anything more. Then again, there are so many ways you can expand upon the basic technique, and a few tricks that make the results truly perfect, so why not let your imagination take charge? ▽

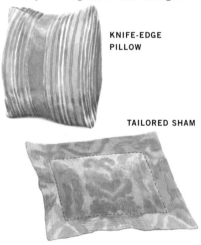

KNIFE-EDGE PILLOW

TAILORED SHAM

MAKING A KNIFE-EDGE PILLOW

To begin, decide the size and shape of your pillow. Generally, a knife-edge pillow will look best if it is filled with a pillow form rather than loose stuffing. With the large variety of forms available in home and sewing stores, it is hardly worth the trouble to make one unless your pillow is an unusual shape. If you do want to make a form, read About Pillow Forms on page 112 and the basic directions that follow.

TIPS FROM THE PROS

✂ Knife-edge pillows can have virtually any outline, but the more complex the outline, the more surprised you may be by the proportions of the finished shape. If you want to make a pillow that is not square or rectangular, it's a good idea to make and stuff a sample before cutting your fabric. Curves and points are particularly deceptive, so test heart shapes or animal silhouettes.

✂ Because their perimeter tends to flute, round knife-edge pillows are possibly the most difficult of all pillow types to sew successfully. One way to minimize the fluting is to align the straight grain of the front with the bias of the back—but this will be obvious if the pattern on the fabric is one like a stripe or check, which ought to match at the edges.

Figuring the Size

It's hard to explain why, but knife-edge pillows don't become smaller when they are stuffed. A piece that is 18" square when flat will still be 18" square when filled; it will always measure 36" around its middle. However, the stuffing does make the pillow plump, so it may appear smaller once filled.

✂ The more you stuff a knife-edge pillow, the more the corners are likely to stand out like pointy dog ears. If you want a simple but really plump pillow, make one with pleated or gathered corners; these are explained in the next section of the book.

In most cases, the pillow cover should be the same size as the form. If you'd prefer a loose-fitting cover, add some ease to the cutting pattern.

✂ Don't assume that a loose cover will give you a relaxed pillow—it's the type of stuffing that makes a pillow squishy, not the fit of the fabric. If you want a fluffy pillow, spring for a down-and-feather form.

Making a Cutting Pattern

Measure your form and draft a pattern of the same dimensions; make it larger for a loose-fitting cover. You can draft on paper or directly onto your fabric. Add $1/2$" seam allowance all around.

✂ If you are making a pillow form, draft a pattern of the desired dimensions and add $1/2$" seam allowance all around.

Cutting the Cover

From the pattern, cut two identical pieces of fabric. Center the pattern over any portion of the fabric you wish to feature, such as a dominant motif or the central portion of a plaid or stripe.

TIPS FROM THE PROS

✂ If you'd like your cover to be easily removable, make it with an overlap closure; refer to Basics, page 117, before cutting.

Sewing the Cover

Place the cut-out pieces right sides together, aligning the cut edges. Pin along the seamline. Sew around the perimeter, pivoting at each corner.

✂ If you are making a pillow form, leave a small opening on one side so you can insert the loose stuffing.

✂ If you are making a cover to go over a form, sew around four corners and three sides, leaving most of the fourth side open so you can insert the form.

Trim the seam allowance at each corner. Press the seam open. Turn the piece right side out. Insert the stuffing or form. Turn in the seam allowance, pin the opening closed, and slipstitch the edges together.

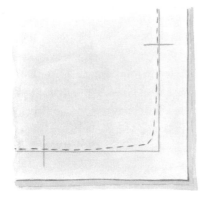

TIPS FROM THE PROS

To minimize pointy, earlike corners, taper the seamline into a sharp curve at each corner instead of sewing a perfect right angle. △

Should you press a sharp fold along the seamed edge after you turn the cover right side out? Generally, no. You want your pillow to have a plump, smooth look; pressing the seam will only encourage it to form a ridge around the pillow perimeter. Depending upon your fabric, the corners might need a little touch-up with an iron.

After turning the pillow cover right side out, insert a blunt-pointed tool through the opening and use it to poke out the corners. A crochet hook is ideal.

If the corners seem too flimsy after you've inserted the form, insert a little loose stuffing between the form and cover at each corner.

MAKING A TAILORED SHAM

A tailored sham must have a back opening so the form can be inserted after the flange is stitched. In other respects, it is made in very much the same way as a basic knife-edge pillow. Refer to page 117 to see how to set up and make an overlap closure.

Cutting the Cover

Draft a pattern with the same dimensions as the form. Decide how deep you'd like the flange to be. Draw a line this distance outside and parallel to the perimeter of the pattern. For the seam allowance, draw another line 1/2" outside this. ▽

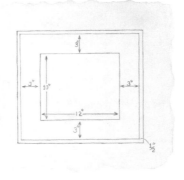

Use the pattern to cut the sham front. Cut out the sham back, making it wider to allow for the overlap closure.

Sewing the Cover

Make the overlap closure. Place the front and back right sides together, aligning the cut edges. Sew together around the perimeter. Trim the corners, press the seam open, and turn the cover right side out. Press the seamed edge sharply. Fasten the back closure.

Using a nonpermanent marker, mark the depth of the flange parallel to the perimeter. Pin the layers together and stitch on the marked line.

DESIGN IDEAS

Knife-edge pillows are such versatile accessories, and so easy to make, that the creative options are endless. In the following pages you'll find directions for eleven projects, some with variations. There is no need to stop with our ideas; they should inspire you to develop your own. Here are a few suggestions.

Embellish, Adapt, or Make an Unusual Fabric

Sew ribbon or lace to the front before sewing the pillow cover together. Use a piece of patchwork, needlepoint, or embroidery; a handkerchief or pretty napkin; a rug or tapestry fragment; or a swatch from a kimono. Dye or paint your own textile.

Add Trim to the Perimeter Seam

That clean outline begs for decoration, and inserting trim or a ruffle into the seam will dress up even the simplest fabrication. Consider matching or contrasting welting, fringe, a double or single pleated or gathered ruffle. ▽

Before sewing the two pieces of the pillow together, baste the desired trim around the perimeter of one of them. On pages 26–28, you'll find detailed directions for adding trim to the seam.

inserted
edging pillows

ABOUT THE SAMPLES

Each of the samples has an important trim inserted in the perimeter seam. The fringe-edged pillow is 22" square; the fabric is silk; the edging is cotton tassel fringe. The ruffle-edged pillow is 20" square with a 2"-deep box-pleated ruffle. The main fabric is rayon voided velvet lined with matching rayon faille. The ruffle is silk organza cut on the bias; the strips are folded in half lengthwise. The triangle-edged pillow is 24" square with a flange of 3³/₄"-deep triangles. The main fabric is rayon moiré with contrasting rayon faille triangles.

MATERIALS

Fabric, as needed for each pillow
Tassel fringe for plaid pillow
Thread to match
Pillow form(s)

TECHNIQUES

Read About Knife-Edge Pillows, pages 24–25. Refer to Part Three, Basics, for information on sewing techniques.

MEASURE, MARK, AND CUT

Note: For the ruffle, cut sufficient bias strips to equal three times the perimeter of the pillow when joined; their width should be twice the desired finished depth plus 1" for the seam allowances. Refer to the directions to make a pattern for the triangles.

Ⓐ **PILLOW FRONT & BACK** ✂cut 2 for each pillow; cut identical pieces from lining, if appropriate

Ⓑ **BIAS STRIPS FOR RUFFLE** ✂cut 5" wide, or as desired

Ⓒ **TRIANGLES** ✂cut 16 from each of two colors

Great colors and dressy fabrics tie together this pair of pillows. Directions for the pillow with the triangles appear on page 28.

FRINGE-EDGED PILLOW

1 Place the pillow front (A) right side up. Place the fringe on it wrong side up; align the straight edge of the fringe header with the cut edge of the pillow front and overlap the ends at the midpoint of one side. You will have to clip the header at each corner. Baste the header to the pillow front. ▷

2 With the right sides together and cut edges aligned, pin and sew the pillow front to the pillow back (A); leave an opening on one side. Trim the seam allowance at each corner and press the seams open. Turn the pillow cover right side out. Insert the pillow form and slipstitch the opening closed.

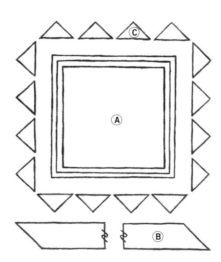

RUFFLE-EDGED PILLOW

TIPS FROM THE PROS

✂Cut the ruffle a little longer than needed, pleat it, and test the fit on the pillow before sewing the ends together.

1 If appropriate, baste the front and back (A) sheer fabric to the lining: Place each lining piece right side up. Aligning the cut edges, place a sheer piece right side up on top of each, and baste together around the perimeter.

2 Sew together the bias strips (B) to form a ring (refer to Basics, page 109). Press the seams open. Fold the strip in half lengthwise, right side out; do not press the fold. Pin and baste the edges together. ▽

3 To prepare for pleating, mark the cut edge at 2" intervals, or at an interval that divides evenly into the finished length of each edge of your pillow. ▽

4 Bring together two consecutive marks and fold the fabric between them to the left. Bring the next mark to meet the first two, and fold the fabric between to the right, forming an inverted box pleat as shown. ▽

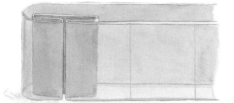

5 Pin the pleat at the cut edge. Continuing in the same manner to bring together three consecutive marks, pleat the rest of the ruffle; do not press.

6 With the cut edges aligned, pin the ruffle to the right side of the pillow front as shown. Clip the ruffle seam allowance at the corners only if necessary. When the pleats fit evenly along each side of the pillow top, baste the entire ruffle in place. ▽

TIPS FROM THE PROS

✂If you've done your math correctly, there will be a pair of marked lines at each corner. If there is not, cheat the pleat spacing as needed.

7 With the right sides together and cut edges aligned, pin and sew the pillow front to the pillow back; leave an opening on one side. To avoid creasing the ruffle, don't press the seam allowance open before turning the pillow cover right side out. Instead, press the seamed edge gently between your fingers after turning. Insert the pillow form and slipstitch the opening closed.

This softly pleated translucent ruffle is a nice complement to the sheer-with-velvet overlay on the pillow body. Try opaque fabrics with crisp pleats for another look.

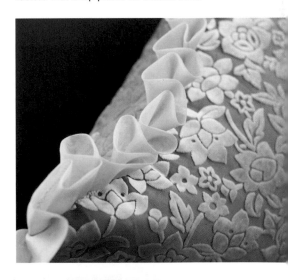

inserted edging pillows

The triangles edging the large pillow are self-lined. You could line them with contrasting fabric or give their edges a decorative finish.

TRIANGLE-EDGED PILLOW

1 On a piece of scrap paper, make a pattern for the triangles (C) as follows: Draw a $7^{1}/_{2}$" square. On it, draw diagonal lines from corner to corner. Draw a $^{1}/_{2}$" seam allowance around one of the triangles just formed. Cut out the triangle pattern on the outer line. ▽

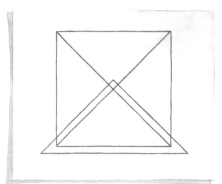

TIPS FROM THE PROS

✄If you're making a different size pillow, you might want to resize the triangle. To do so, determine the desired length of the hypotenuse (the edge sewn to the pillow), and substitute that dimension for the $7^{1}/_{2}$" in the above directions. The hypotenuse of the triangles in the sample is one-quarter the length of the pillow edge, plus $1^{1}/_{2}$" for overlap.

✄To equalize bias distortion, cut the triangles with the hypotenuse on the straight grain of the fabric. When you sew the triangles, try not to stretch the bias edges.

2 Cut out the triangles as directed. With the right sides together and cut edges aligned, pin each triangle to one of the same color. Sew the paired triangles together along the short edges; leave the long edge (hypotenuse) open. ◁

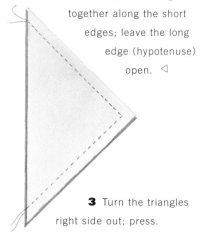

3 Turn the triangles right side out; press.

4 Place the pillow front (A) right side up. Aligning the cut edges and alternating colors, pin four triangles to each edge: Overlap the triangles along each edge but make sure the seamed edges butt at each corner of the pillow top. Baste the triangles in place. ▽

5 With the right sides together and cut edges aligned, pin and sew the pillow front to the pillow back (A); leave an opening on one side. Trim the seam allowance at each corner and press the seams open. Turn the pillow cover right side out. Insert the pillow form and slipstitch the opening closed.

channel-quilted shams

FOR BOTH SHAMS

1 Place the sham front (A) wrong side up and top with a piece of batting, then with a piece of lining. Pin the layers together and baste along the seamlines. ▽

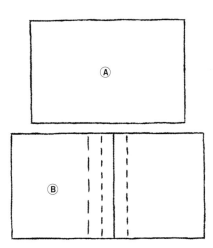

2 To set up the overlap closure, cut the sham back (B) into two pieces (refer to Basics, page 117). Press the hem allowance to the wrong side of each piece along the overlap edge.

These tailored shams would also look great sized up for bed pillows. Their tops are backed with batting and then channel-quilted before being sewn to the backs. Follow our quilting suggestions or use a pattern of your own.

ABOUT THE SAMPLES

The pillow shams are made from cotton damask backed with batting. The front of each is quilted. The sham with the fringed edge is 12" x 18"; plan to center a tassel at each corner. The sham with the fringe applied over the flange is 14" x 20", including a 2"-deep flange; plan to center a space between tassels at each corner. Plan the size of your sham so any color repeat on the tassel fringe works out evenly.

MATERIALS

Fabric
Tassel fringe
Batting
Muslin underlining
Thread to match
Buttons or desired fastener for back closure
Pillow form(s)

TECHNIQUES

Read About Knife-Edge Pillows, pages 24–25. Refer to Part Three, Basics, for information on overlap closures and other sewing techniques.

MEASURE, MARK, AND CUT

Note: Cut the sham back wide enough to allow for an overlap closure. For each piece, cut an identical piece of batting and lining.

Ⓐ **SHAM FRONT** ✄ cut 1 for each pillow
Ⓑ **SHAM BACK** ✄ cut 1 for each pillow

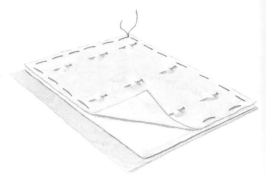

3 Place the sham backs wrong side up and unfold the hem allowance. Top each piece with a piece of batting, then with a piece of lining; align the batting and lining with the foldline of the hem allowances. Pin the layers together, trim the batting and lining even with the outer edges of the backs, and baste together along the seamlines. ▷

4 Pin the hems over the linings and topstitch to secure. If desired, make buttonholes in the hem of one back (refer to Basics, page 121); or sew corresponding pieces of hook-and-loop tape to the inside of one hem and to the outside of the other.

FOR THE FRINGE-EDGED PILLOW

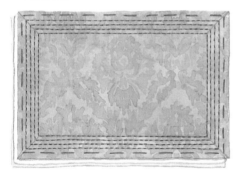

1 Place the sham front right side up. Using chalk or nonpermanent marking pen, draw a 45-degree line from each corner to the center. Draw four concentric lines $^3/_8$" apart inside the perimeter basting line. Starting on one side, stitch along one of the lines through all layers; pivot at each corner. Repeat on each remaining line. △

TIPS FROM THE PROS

✂Use a 45-degree right-angle triangle and a transparent gridded ruler to set up the quilting lines.

✂To prevent the layers from creeping, sew with an even-feed or walking foot on your machine.

✂Be sure the needle is piercing the fabric when you lift the presser foot to pivot at the corners.

2 Place the sham front right side up. Place the fringe on it wrong side up, aligning the tasseled edge of the fringe header with the basting line and facing the tassels toward the sham center. Position a tassel at each corner and overlap the ends of the header on one edge; you will have to clip the header at each corner. Baste the header to the sham front through all the layers. ▽

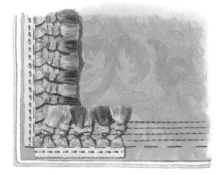

TIPS FROM THE PROS

✂Use a liquid fray retardent to keep the clipped and overlapped ends of the tassel header from raveling.

✂To reduce bulk, be sure the header overlap won't coincide with the back opening.

3 Place the sham backs right side up and overlap the hemmed edges; be sure the appropriate one is on top. Pin together at each end of the overlap. Place the sham front wrong side up on top of the back and pin them together. Trim any excess length from the back. Sew the front and back together.

4 Trim the batting from the seam allowances and trim the seam allowance at each corner. Press the seams open. Turn the sham right side out. Press along the edges to smooth the seam but don't make a sharp crease. Pin the sham front to the sham back along the inner quilting line, and stitch together through all layers where pinned.

5 If the overlap has buttonholes, sew a button to the underlap opposite each. Insert the pillow form and fasten the closure.

FOR THE APPLIED FRINGE PILLOW

1 Refer to the photograph as you mark the concentric quilting pattern on the right side of the sham front. Using chalk and a square, center and draw a rectangle a little larger than your pillow form on the sham front. Where the lines meet, draw a 45-degree line inward from each corner. Draw a line parallel to and halfway between the longer sides of the rectangle. Draw additional lines parallel to both sides of this line, placing them at $3/8$" intervals and stopping them at the angled lines; make the last line about 1" inside the rectangle. ▽

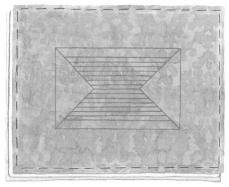

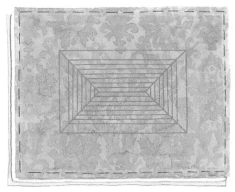

2 Measure the distance between the rectangle and the last line drawn. Draw a line this distance inside and parallel to each end of the rectangle, completing another rectangle. Draw additional lines parallel to and inside the rectangle ends, placing them at $3/8$" intervals. Brush off any overlapping lines to reveal the concentric rectangles. Adjust the first line drawn in the center so it stops $3/8$" from the ends of the inner rectangle. △

3 Stitch on the center line through all layers. Working from the center out, stitch on the marked rectangles; start stitching on one side of each and pivot at each corner. Do not stitch the outermost rectangle.

4 Place the sham backs right side up and overlap the hemmed edges; be sure the appropriate one is on top. Pin together at each end of the overlap. Place the sham front wrong side up on top of the back and pin them together. Sew the front and back together.

Dressy tassel fringe gives a formal finish to this cotton damask sham. You could also use ball fringe or a simple cut fringe like that shown on page 58.

5 Trim the batting from the seam allowances and trim the seam allowance at each corner. Press the seams open. Turn the sham right side out. Press along the edges to smooth the seam but don't make a sharp crease. Pin the sham front to the back along the remaining marked rectangle and stitch together through all layers.

6 Place the sham right side up. Place the fringe on it right side up, with the tassels facing out, aligning the tasseled edge of the header just inside the last line of stitching. Overlapping the ends of the header on one side, position a space between tassels at each corner, folding a miter into the header. ▽

7 Pin or baste the fringe header to the sham and slipstitch into place.

8 If the overlap has buttonholes, sew a button to the underlap opposite each. Insert the pillow form and fasten the closure.

flanged pillows

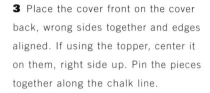

ABOUT THE SAMPLES

These pillows are made by sandwiching pillow forms between layers of fabric; the layers are sewn together next to the forms. The edges of each piece of fabric are finished with serging. One pillow is covered in lightweight velvet, the other in lightweight opaque silk topped with semisheer textured silk. The velvet pillow is 21" x 27", including a 3"-deep flange all around. The silk pillow is 18" x 24", including a 3"-deep flange all around.

MATERIALS

Fabric(s)
4 tasseled tiebacks or cording and 8 tassels for each pillow
Rayon machine-embroidery thread
Thread to match
Pillow form(s)

TECHNIQUES

Read About Knife-Edge Pillows, pages 24–25. Refer to Part Three, Basics, for information on sewing techniques. Before cutting the pieces, refer to the Designer Detail on page 34 for ideas for finishing the edges.

MEASURE, MARK, AND CUT

Note: Measure the length of your pillow form and add twice the finished flange depth to it. Measure the width of your pillow form and add twice the finished flange depth to it. For each cover, cut two pieces of these dimensions. Cut the topper sufficiently smaller to reveal a margin of the underlying fabric.

Ⓐ **COVER FRONT & BACK** ✂cut 2 for each pillow

Ⓑ **COVER TOPPER** ✂cut 1

1 Finish the edges of each piece of fabric (refer to the Designer Detail, page 34).

2 If you are making the pillow with the topper (B), place the topper right side up. If you are not, place the cover front (A) right side up. Using chalk, and a square, draw a rectangle the size of your pillow form centered on the topper or cover front. ▽

TIPS FROM THE PROS

✂The easiest way to center the rectangle is by marking a line parallel to and the depth of the flange from each edge. Use a transparent gridded ruler as a guide.

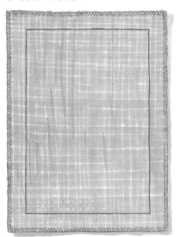

Ⓐ   Ⓑ

3 Place the cover front on the cover back, wrong sides together and edges aligned. If using the topper, center it on them, right side up. Pin the pieces together along the chalk line.

4 Sew the pieces together on the marked line, leaving one end open. ▽

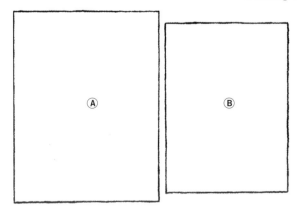

TIPS FROM THE PROS

✂If sewing velvet, avoid misaligned pieces by hand basting the layers together before sewing. Then sew by hand, using small stitches, or by machine, using a walking foot.

5 Insert the pillow form between the cover front and back. Pin and sew the remaining end closed (use a zipper foot if sewing by machine).

Nothing could be easier to make than these pretty pillows—just choose fabric with a soft hand so the corners will drape nicely. You could adapt these directions to make a knife-edge pillow of almost any shape.

6 Center a tieback over the stitches on each edge of the pillow form. Whipstitch the cord to the pillow cover; at each corner secure the stitches and leave the extending cord loose. ▷

TIPS FROM THE PROS

✄ You can sew the cord to nonpile woven fabric by machine. Use a grooved cording foot, guide the cord under the center of the foot, and sew it on using a wide, long zigzag stitch.

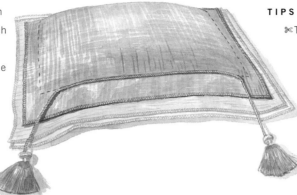

7 Knot the extending cord at each corner and tack each knot to the cover.

TIPS FROM THE PROS

✄ To shorten the tiebacks, slide the tassel up the cord; tape or knot the cord in a new place and cut off the excess.

✄ If you are assembling your own tasseled cords, thread the cord through the loop on the tassel, fold the end back on itself and wrap with matching thread. Or knot the end of the cord and sew the tassel to the knot.

decorative edge finishes

The edges of our pillows were finished with a serger, but there are other ways you can finish them. In fact, different fabrics can be enhanced by different finishes. Whichever technique you choose, test it by making a sample on a piece of your pillow cover fabric; be sure to sew around a corner. If you decide on a technique that turns the hem, be sure to add the appropriate hem allowance to your pieces when you cut them out.

SERGED FINISH

This technique works when the fabric is cut to the finished dimensions; do not trim the edges while serging.

✂ Use a three-thread balanced stitch formation with the right needle threaded.

✂ Use cotton or polyester thread in the right needle and rayon machine-embroidery thread in the upper and lower loopers. If you wish, use three colors.

1 Begin stitching on one side of each piece. When you reach a corner, stop stitching and raise the needle and presser foot. With your finger, pull out the thread above the needle eye to create about $1/2$" slack (or, if this is not possible, as much as your serger will permit), pivot the fabric, lower the presser foot, and continue stitching. Repeat at each corner.

2 When you return to the starting point, serge over the previous stitches for about $1/2$", then stitch a 6"-long tail off to the side. Cut the threads, leaving the tail attached to the fabric.

3 Thread the tail through a crewel needle and slide it under the serging on the wrong side of the fabric for about 1". Cut off the excess tail.

SEWING MACHINE FINISHES

✂ Experiment with the different finishing stitches on your machine to find one that works with your fabric. Consult your operating manual for thread suggestions.

✂ Try an overlock stitch to approximate the look of the serged finish.

✂ Use a baby-hem rolling foot to make a narrow hem. Try it with a narrow zigzag stitch for a more decorative look.

✂ Make a stitch-turn-stitch baby hem (refer to Basics, page 115).

✂ Try a buttonhole foot and a narrow zigzag stitch; the fabric edge may roll under, forming a tiny hem.

Choose thread that matches or contrasts the fabric to finish the edges. If you're up for a challenge, consider scalloping the fabric edges—some machines can be programmed to embroider large scallops or other designs.

HANDMADE FINISHES

✂ Overcast the edges by hand (consult an embroidery manual for a pretty stitch).

✂ Make a tiny rolled hem by hand.

✂ Finish the edges with a bead of decorative fabric paint.

✂ Fringe the edges.

✂ Cut a decorative edge with pinking or scalloping shears—especially nice if the pillows are made from felt.

ribbon-embroidered pillow

TIPS FROM THE PROS

✂ The easiest way to prepare this sham is to cut the front somewhat larger than needed, stitch the embroidery, and then cut the front to size. This will allow you some leeway in plotting your embroidery pattern. Cut the sham back after the embroidery is complete.

✂ If you use an evenweave fabric (one with the same number of threads per inch in each direction), you can stitch over the same number of threads for each repeat of the pattern.

This bold embroidery has a wonderful, almost primitive, appeal. Make this pillow in multiples, reversing the color of cloth and ribbon on some.

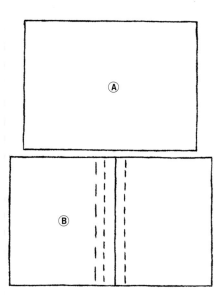

ABOUT THE SAMPLE

The pillow sham is made from raw silk monk's cloth; the front is embroidered with rayon seam tape. The sham is 16" x 23", not including a 1¼"-deep fringed flange. Each tab portion of the embroidery design is about 2" wide.

MATERIALS

Fabric
Rayon seam tape
Fusible interfacing (small amount)
Thread to match
Buttons or desired fastener for back closure
Pillow form

TECHNIQUES

Read About Knife-Edge Pillows, pages 24–25. Refer to Part Three, Basics, for information on overlap closures and other sewing techniques.

MEASURE, MARK, AND CUT

Note: Cut the sham back wide enough to allow for an overlap closure. Refer to the tip preceding the directions before cutting the pieces.

Ⓐ **SHAM FRONT** ✂ cut 1
Ⓑ **SHAM BACK** ✂ cut 1

graphic ribbon-embroidered pillow

1 Referring to the Designer Detail opposite, embroider the sham front (A). Trim the excess fabric about 1¹/₂" beyond the outer edge of the ribbon, or to accommodate the desired fringe length.

2 Make an overlap closure on the sham back (B), trimming the back to the same size as the front, applying the fastening, and pinning the overlap closed at the hem ends (refer to Basics, page 117).

3 Cut eight strips of stable fusible interfacing 1" wide; make four strips 2" shorter than the long edges of the sham and four 4" shorter than the short edges. Pin a strip parallel to and about 1" inside each long edge of the sham front and back; don't place the interfacing across the hems but trim the excess. Then pin a strip between the first two, parallel to and 1" inside each short end. Fuse the interfacing in place. ▽

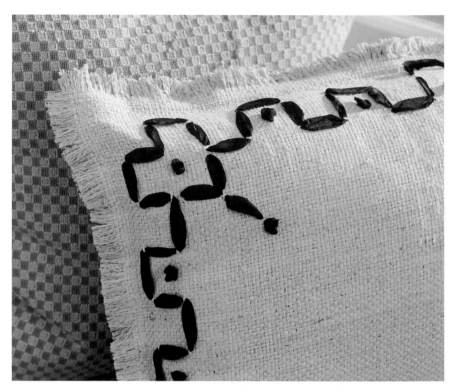

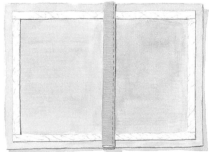

4 Check that the sham back hems are overlapped properly. Place the pinned-together backs wrong side up. With the cut edges aligned, place the sham front right side up on top of the backs. Pin and sew together 1¹/₄" inside the cut edges; use a medium zigzag stitch and be sure to sew through the interfacing.

5 On each edge of the sham front and back, remove the parallel threads to create a fringe about 1" deep. ▷

TIPS FROM THE PROS
✂When fringing, work first on one edge, then on the opposite edge, then, one at a time, on the adjacent edges.

You can make this pillow in any size. If you make it smaller, use fewer repeats of the pattern at this scale or consider adjusting the scale of the fabric weave and the ribbon width to maintain their proportion to the overall size—this will give a surprisingly different, more delicate look.

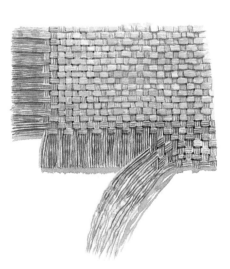

geometric ribbon embroidery

This informal bold embroidery is a combination of long straight stitches, woven under a single thread of the fabric, and loose French knots. The spacing of the pattern doesn't have to be absolutely perfect to be effective. You can duplicate our pattern or create one of your own.

1 Plan your embroidery pattern by drawing it to scale on graph paper. To ensure that the corners are symmetrical, each side of the pattern must begin and end with a tab.▽

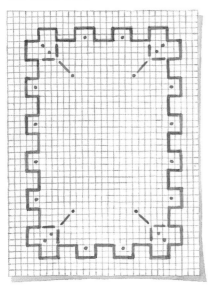

TIPS FROM THE PROS

✂ Before drawing the entire pattern, stitch one or two repeats on a scrap of your fabric. Because the ribbon floats loosely over the fabric, the symmetry of the pattern may not emerge exactly as you anticipate. The tabs on the sham in the photo appear as deep as they are wide, but in fact they are a bit shallower.

2 Mark the sham front at the appropriate intervals with guidelines for the top and bottom of the embroidery pattern. Do this by basting two lines in a contrasting color thread or by adhering quilter's masking tape (refer to Basics, page 123). If you wish, you can also mark the tab width along the outer guideline.

3 Thread a large tapestry needle (large eye, blunt tip) with rayon seam tape. Stitch the tab border first, passing the needle under one thread of the fabric at each turn in the design. △

TIPS FROM THE PROS

✂ Do not knot the seam tape; leave any loose ends on the wrong side and tie them together when you are finished with all the embroidery.

4 Next stitch the inner corner pattern, including both French knots, then the individual French knots in the tabs.

✂ To make a French knot, bring the needle up from the wrong side of the fabric, wrap the seam tape around it twice, reinsert the needle close to the point where it emerged, and pull it through to the wrong side; keep the wrapped tape close to the fabric with the thumb of your other hand, forming a loose knot. ▽

pillow slip

ABOUT THE SAMPLES

The sample is made from coordinating striped and tweed denim. The slip is 18" x 24"; it holds an 18"-square pillow form. Pairs of linked buttons close the cuff. Use one, two, or three fabrics, orienting any stripes as you wish. You'll see a 24" x 30" version of this pillow on page 59.

MATERIALS

Fabric(s)
Cable cord for welting
Buttons
Thread to match
Pillow form

TECHNIQUES

Read About Knife-Edge Pillows, pages 24–25. Refer to Part Three, Basics, for information on sewing techniques.

MEASURE, MARK, AND CUT

Note: Cut the cuff in one piece, making it twice as wide as the slip and twice the desired finished depth. Add seam allowance to all edges of each piece.

Ⓐ **PILLOW SLIP FRONT & BACK** ✂cut 2
Ⓑ **BIAS STRIPS** ✂cut 1³⁄₄" x twice the width of the slip
Ⓒ **CUFF** ✂cut 1

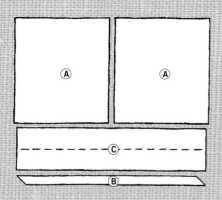

1 With the right sides together and cut edges aligned, sew the slip front (A) to the slip back (A); leave one end open. Trim the corners, finish the seam edges, and turn the slip right side out.

2 Make the piping (B). With right sides together and cut edges aligned, baste the piping to the open end of the slip. Finish the piping ends neatly (refer to Basics, pages 118–19). ▽

TIPS FROM THE PROS

✂Join the piping somewhere along the open edge of the slip, not on one of the seams.

3 Sew the ends of the cuff together to make a ring. Press the seam open. ▽

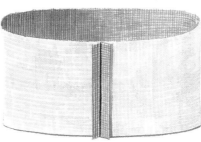

This pillow slip is open at one end just like a bed pillowcase; the cuffed end folds over to give it square proportions. Consider making this in dressier fabric and trim or make it very small to hold a scented pillow.

4 Fold the cuff in half lengthwise, right side out, and press. Finish one edge (see Basics, page 114). ▽

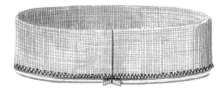

5 Unfold the cuff. Slide it, wrong side out, over the right side of the slip; align the cuff seam with one seam on the slip. Pin the cuff to the slip and, using a zipper foot or piping foot, sew together along the piping basting line. ▽

✂Keep the slip right side out and sew around the inside.

6 Fold the cuff away from the slip and press the seam toward the cuff. Fold the cuff in half again along the crease made in step 4, covering the seam allowance and lapping the finished edge over the seamline. Pin or baste.

7 Turn the slip wrong side out and stitch the cuff through all layers right next to the piping. Turn the cuff right side out and press. ▽

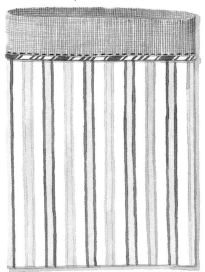

8 Place the slip flat on your worktable. Referring to the photographs, measure and mark evenly spaced buttonholes on the top cuff layer. Turn the slip over and duplicate the marks on the other cuff layer. Make the buttonholes (refer to Basics, page 121).

9 Make cufflink buttons by sewing two buttons together, joining them with a ¹/₂"-long thread shank. Wrap the thread around the shank several times, pass it once again through one button, and slide the needle under the wraps before knotting the thread or securing it with a few stitches; then cut the excess thread. ▽

✂Before making the complete set of cufflinks, make one and insert it through the cuff to test the length of the shank.

10 Insert the pillow form in the slip. Insert the cufflinks. Fold the cuff to one side, allowing it to relax over the form.

To achieve the full benefit of this relaxed design, use a down-filled form in your pillow slip. If you have 24"-square pillows on your bed, cover them with a pair of these slips instead of classic European shams.

miter-banded pillow shams

ABOUT THE SAMPLES

Both shams are printed cotton trimmed with a metallic sheer. The large sham is 24" square; it is trimmed with $3^1/_2$"-wide mesh ribbon. The small sham is $12^1/_2$" square with a $2^1/_2$"-deep flange made of 6"-wide crinkled metallic organza ribbon. If you wish to substitute fabric for ribbon, finish the edges appropriately on the large sham.

MATERIALS

Fabric
Ribbon(s)
Fastener for back closure
Thread to match
Pillow form(s)

TECHNIQUES

Read About Knife-Edge Pillows, pages 24–25. Refer to Part Three, Basics, for information on overlap closures and other sewing techniques.

MEASURE, MARK, AND CUT

Note: Cut each sham back wide enough to allow for an overlap closure. To calculate the amount of ribbon needed for the small sham flange, add twice the finished flange depth (5" in the sample) to the sham size ($12^1/_2$") to find the length of the outermost edge of the pillow ($17^1/_2$"); multiply by four (70") and add 8" to allow for seams and ease of handling.

- Ⓐ **LARGE SHAM BACK** ✂cut 1
- Ⓑ **LARGE SHAM FRONT** ✂cut 1
- Ⓒ **LARGE SHAM RIBBON BAND** ✂cut 4, each the same length as the cut side of the front
- Ⓓ **SMALL SHAM BACK** ✂cut 1
- Ⓔ **SMALL SHAM FRONT** ✂cut 1
- Ⓕ **SMALL SHAM RIBBON FLANGE** ✂cut the ribbon into 4 equal pieces

LARGE SHAM

1 Make the overlap closure on the sham back (A), trimming the back to the same size as the front (B), applying the fastening, and pinning the overlap closed at the hem ends (refer to Basics, page 117).

2 Place the ribbons (C) wrong side up. Center and mark the finished length of the sham side on one edge of each. Using a 45-degree right-angle triangle, draw a diagonal line from the mark at each end to the other edge; the lines should slant in opposite directions. ▽

3 With the right sides together and all edges aligned, sew one end of one ribbon to the end of another on the marked line. Repeat, joining the ribbons into a square frame with mitered corners. Center the frame on the sham front and check the fit—the outer edge of the ribbon should sit $1/_2$" inside the cut edge of the fabric—adjust if necessary. △

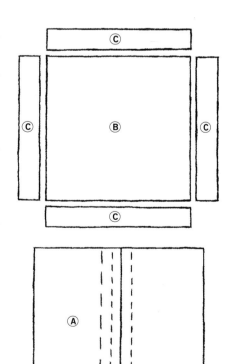

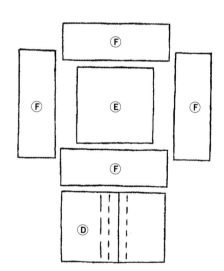

4 Lift the ribbon and trim the mitered seam allowances to $1/4"$; press each to one side. Reposition the frame on the sham front, pin, and sew in place along both edges of the ribbon.

TIPS FROM THE PROS

✄If your ribbon has raised edges, try sewing it to the sham front using a grooved pin-tuck presser foot; position one of the grooves over the ribbon edge.

5 Place the sham back right side up. Place the sham front wrong side up on top of it. Pin and sew together around the perimeter, stitching just outside the outer line of stitching on the sham front.

6 Trim the seam allowance at the corners and press the seams open. Turn the sham right side out. If the overlap has buttonholes, sew a button opposite each on the underlap. Insert the pillow form and fasten the closure.

SMALL SHAM

1 Make the overlap closure on the sham back (D), trimming the back to the same size as the front (E), applying the fastening, and pinning the overlap closed at the hem ends (refer to Basics, page 117).

2 With the wrong sides together and cut edges aligned, sew the sham front to the sham back along the perimeter.

3 To prepare the ribbon flange (F), press each ribbon piece in half lengthwise, right side out. Then press $1/2"$ to the wrong side along one edge. ▽

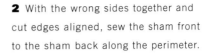

4 With right sides together, center and pin one piece of ribbon to one edge of the front of the sham; align the ribbon edge that is not pressed under with the cut edge of the sham. Sew on the ribbon; do not stitch into the adjacent seam allowance at each end. ▽

Two classic pillow shams feature mitered borders. Here metallic ribbon frames a strong motif, but these designs can be effective in many fabrications.

miter-banded pillow shams

5 Repeat to sew a piece of ribbon to each remaining side of the sham.

6 Place the sham on the table with the front up. Fold it in half diagonally, so the back faces you. Fold the ribbons away from the sham, aligning the seamlines and folds. Align one leg of a 45-degree right-angle triangle with the fold across the sham back and place the corner on the lengthwise fold in the middle of the ribbon, as shown. Draw a right angle on the ribbon, following the triangle. Remove the triangle, pin the ribbons together on the line. Repeat at the opposite corner. ▽

Whether you topstitch the border to the pillow front or apply it as a soft flange, you can make either style of pillow sham in whatever size you wish.

7 To miter the pinned corners, sew on the marked lines. Then put the sham back on the table, fold diagonally in the opposite direction, and mark, pin, and sew the remaining corners.

TIPS FROM THE PROS
✂ For best results, fold the seam allowance at the edge of the sham out of the way when sewing the miters; don't stitch through it.

8 Trim the excess ribbon from the mitered seams; press them open. Trim the seam allowance around the sham perimeter, and press it toward the ribbon flange. At each corner, turn the flange right side out. Align the folded edge with the seamline; pin and slipstitch. ▷

9 If the overlap has buttonholes, sew a button opposite each on the underlap. Insert the pillow form and fasten the closure.

fold-over
envelope sham

1 To calculate the size to cut the sham, measure one edge of your pillow form. On scrap paper, draw a line this length. Use a 45-degree right-angle triangle to draw a 45-degree line at each end; extend the lines so they intersect, forming a right-angle triangle. Measure one leg of the triangle, and multiply by 2. Cut the fabric squares for the sham (A) twice this size, adding seam allowance all around. ▽

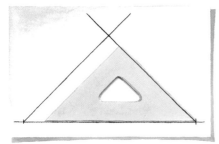

TIPS FROM THE PROS

✂ You can figure the sham size mathematically. The length of the pillow form edge is the hypotenuse of the fold-over triangles. Calculate the square of the hypotenuse and divide by 2. Find the square root of the resulting number and multiply by 2. Cut the fabric squares to this size, plus seam allowance.

This clever pillow cover is just a large square of fabric—lined and with piping around the edges—folded up envelope style. The bottom point is sewn to the side points and the top ties closed, although you could use loops and buttons if you prefer.

ABOUT THE SAMPLE

The sham is a large square with each corner folded to the center to make an envelope. The cotton gingham print is piped, lined, and tied with solid red cotton. The pillow form is 16" square. If you wish, make a simple knife-edge cover for your form, as it will show between the tied edges of the sham.

MATERIALS

Fabric(s)
Cable cord, narrow for ties and piping
Thread to match
Pillow form

TECHNIQUES

Read About Knife-Edge Pillows, pages 24–25. Refer to Part Three, Basics, for information on sewing techniques.

MEASURE, MARK, AND CUT

Note: Refer to step 1 and the tip following it to calculate the size to cut the sham.

(A) SHAM ✂ cut 1 each from outer fabric and lining

(B) BIAS STRIPS ✂ cut 1¹/₂" wide, sufficient to rim perimeter of sham and make 6 ties, each 12" long

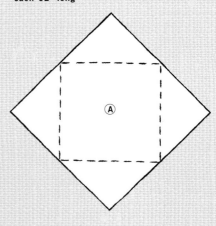

fold-over envelope sham

2 Referring to the Designer Detail, opposite, make six 12" tubular ties from the bias strips (B); begin by cutting six 2' lengths of cable cord.

3 Place the outer fabric square right side up. Divide the length of the edge by 4; on two adjacent edges, make a mark this distance from each corner. With the cut edges aligned, sew a tie at each mark and at two opposite corners, as shown. ▷

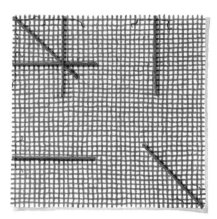

4 Make the piping from the bias strips (B). With the right sides together and cut edges aligned, machine baste the piping to the perimeter of the sham. Finish the ends neatly. (Refer to Basics, pages 118–19.) ▽

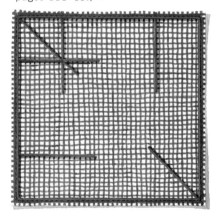

Covered-cording ties match the piping around the envelope edges.

5 With the right sides together and cut edges aligned, sew the piped square to the lining, leaving an opening on one edge. Trim the corners, turn the sham right side out, slipstitch the opening closed, and press.

TIPS FROM THE PROS
 To keep the ties away from the seam, pin them to the center of the piped square before sewing it to the lining.

6 Place the sham lining side up. Fold the bottom and side corners to the center as shown. ▽

7 Pin the adjacent diagonal edges together through the piping seams. Using a zipper foot or piping foot, sew the pinned seams; stitch from each bottom corner to the center. Be sure to backstitch at each end—these seams will receive some stress when you insert the form. ▽

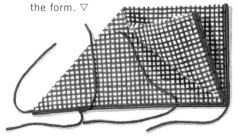

8 Insert the pillow form, fold the top triangle to the center, and tie each tie in a bow. If desired, knot the end of each tie and cut off any excess.

covered cording

Covered cording can be used as a decorative trim or to make ties. The technique is a bit tricky, but once you get the hang of it, it's easy. Once the cording is turned, you can leave the cord itself inside or pull it out to leave a flat tube. For each length of covered cording you wish to make, cut a piece of cable cord twice the desired finished length. You must use bias strips for the covering.

TIPS FROM THE PROS

✄ Don't try to make more than a 3' length at one time; if you need more, make several individual lengths.

✄ Making covered cording from napped fabrics such as velveteen is difficult because they stick to the cord, and so are hard to turn. Try using rattail instead of cotton cable cord, and don't cover it too tightly.

1 Place the zipper foot or piping foot on your machine, positioning it to the left of the needle.

2 Wrap the bias strip wrong side out around the cord, placing one end of the bias at the midpoint of the cord.

3 Sew across the end of the strip, sewing through the cord and for a couple of stitches beyond it. Pivot and, stitching close to the cord, continue sewing until the rest of the cord is enclosed. △

4 Turn the bias strip right side out over the cord: Begin at the middle, where the bias strip is stitched across the cord. Trim the seam allowance at this point and then, using your fingers, ease the bias strip gently over itself toward the exposed cord. Once the bias strip turns over the crosswise seam, hold the cord extending from the open end of the bias strip firmly in one hand and, with your other hand, continue to ease the bias strip down over itself; the bias strip will slide easily over the remainder of the cord. ▷

5 Trim the excess cord close to the stitched end.

✄ If you wish to close the opposite end of the cording, cut the cord about $1/4$" inside the end, hand gather the bias covering, and tuck it inside, pulling the gathers tight.

✄ If you wish to remove the cord, clip off the closed end and pull the cord out from inside.

geometric pillows

ABOUT THE SAMPLES

Each pillow is covered in cotton print, has contrasting ruched welting inserted at the perimeter, and is tufted at the center and trimmed with a covered button. The round pillow is 16½" in diameter; the square pillow is 15" on each side; the triangular pillow is 18" on each side.

MATERIALS

Fabric for each pillow cover
Contrasting fabric for ruched welting
Contrasting fabric for button
Cable cord for welting
Button forms to cover
Thread to match
Heavy thread for tufting
Pillow form for each pillow

TECHNIQUES

Read About Knife-Edge Pillows, pages 24–25. Refer to Part Three, Basics, for information on sewing techniques.

MEASURE, MARK, AND CUT

Note: To draft the patterns, refer to step 1. Cut the bias strips for the welting a little wider than usual so you can slide it easily over the cord; for each pillow, cut enough strips to equal about twice the perimeter.

Ⓐ **ROUND PILLOW FRONT & BACK** ✂cut 2
Ⓑ **SQUARE PILLOW FRONT & BACK** ✂cut 2
Ⓒ **TRIANGULAR PILLOW FRONT & BACK** ✂cut 2
Ⓓ **BIAS STRIPS** ✂cut sufficient to make ruched piping to rim each pillow

1 Draft the patterns for the pillows. You can draw them directly onto the fabric or onto a piece of paper first.
✂Draft a circle of the desired size, including seam allowance (refer to Basics, page 110).
✂Use an L-square to mark a square of the desired size; add seam allowance.
✂For the triangle, draw a line 2" longer than the desired length of the pillow side. Mark both ends and the midpoint. Using an L-square, draw a line perpendicular to the midpoint. Between this line and each marked end of the first line, draw a line the same length as the first line. Round the points of the triangle. Rule ½" seam allowance around this shape. ▽

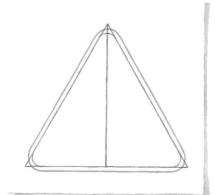

TIPS FROM THE PROS

✂It is difficult to judge the proportions of a set of differently shaped pillows such as these. For best results, make a sample of each in muslin, stuff and tuft it, and then look at them all together. If you like the set, undo the tufting, and use them as the pillow forms.
✂Once you've cut out the pillow covers, fuse a scrap of interfacing to the center of each piece to reinforce it for tufting later.

2 For each pillow, sew together the bias strips, making a ring twice the perimeter of your pillow (refer to Basics, page 109). Cut a length of cord several inches longer than the perimeter of the pillow.

3 Place a zipper foot on your machine, adjusting it so the foot is to the right of the needle. Wrap the bias strip, right side out, over the cord, aligning the cut edges; secure the end of the bias strip to the end of the cord with a safety pin. Sew the bias strip together next to the cord, but not so close that the cover is tight.

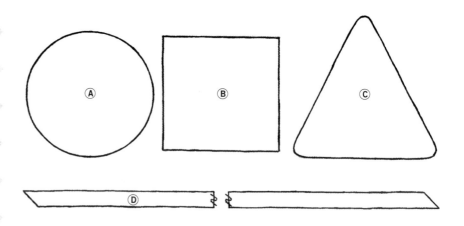

4 After sewing for 10"–12", stop with the needle in the fabric. Lift the presser foot and pull the cord toward you, ruching (gathering) the stitched portion of the fabric over the cord. ▽

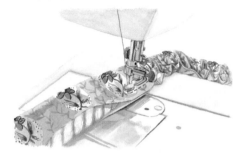

5 Lower the presser foot, sew another 10"–12", and pull the cord again. In this manner, continue until all but 3" of cord have been covered and about 6" of bias strip is still loose. To maintain the tension while you apply the welting to the project, secure the end of the ruched section to the cord with a safety pin.

TIPS FROM THE PROS

✄ You can make the ruching in whatever proportion pleases you. Make a sample before cutting and joining all the bias strips, or wait to join the ends of the bias strips into a ring until you've covered the cord and pulled up the ruche to the desired fullness.

✄ If you have a leather roller foot for your machine, use it when sewing the ruching; it allows just the right amount of space between the needle and the cord (see Basics, page 125).

These shapely pillows will change character with the fabric you choose—they'd be quite elegant in velvet and satin with corded trim. For best results, use a down-filled form.

tufted geometric pillows

6 With the right sides together and cut edges aligned, sew the ruched welting to the edges of each pillow front. Begin and end in the middle of one side, not at a corner; leave the welting free at the cord ends.

7 Place each pillow front right side up. Fold the seam allowance under, onto the wrong side, so the welting turns out to rim the perimeter. Make sure it lies smoothly around the perimeter; pull the cord tighter if it waffles; ease it into the covering if it binds. ▽

8 Trim the ends of the cord so they butt and tack them together. ▽

The ruched welting adds a pleasing dimensional finish to these button-tufted pillows. To minimize bulk in the seam, choose a lightweight fabric for the ruching.

9 Wrap the loose portion of the bias strip over the cord to cover the joint, pin it to the pillow front, easing in the fullness, and complete the seam.

10 With the right sides together and cut edges aligned, pin each pillow front to the corresponding pillow back. Sew together, stitching just inside the previous stitching; leave an opening large enough to insert the pillow form.

TIPS FROM THE PROS
✂The ruched welting tends to be bulky. For better control, baste the back to the front before sewing them together.

11 Trim the bulk from the corners of the triangular and square pillow covers. Turn the pillow covers right side out. Press the perimeter seam of each. Insert the pillow forms and slipstitch the openings closed.

12 Cover the button forms. Thread a sturdy needle with heavy thread. Insert the needle all the way through the center of one of the pillows, pull it through, leaving a long tail of thread on both sides, and remove the needle. Repeat about $1/4$" away. On one side of the pillow, tie a square knot; leave the long thread tails hanging. Repeat on the other side, pulling the thread tight to indent the pillow.

13 On one side of the pillow, pass one thread end through a button shank and tie securely to the other thread end. Cut off the excess threads. Repeat on the other side.

TIPS FROM THE PROS
✂The thread tying the pillow at the center will be under stress. Use very sturdy thread—the waxed variety sometimes used to string beads is ideal.

back-to-front shams

There's no reason to hide the overlap closure on a pillow sham—on this pair it moves front and not quite center. Whether you use up those scraps you can't bear to toss or start fresh, think of solids and textures as well as prints.

END-BAND SHAM

TIPS FROM THE PROS

✂ The easiest way to prepare this sham is to cut the back a little long and size it as explained in steps 4 and 5 on the next page.

1 Fold the button band (A) in half lengthwise, right side out, and press. Finish one long edge. ▽

2 Sew the unfinished edge of the band to the end of the sham front (B). Fold the band away from the front and press the seam toward the band. ▽

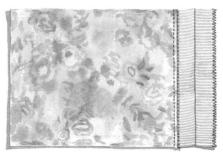

ABOUT THE SAMPLES

Each section of these shams is cut from a different print. The sham with the button band at the end is 12" x 18"; the end of the back extends and folds over to become the button underlap, forming a pocket to hold the pillow form. The sham with the button band more to the middle is 10" x 14".

MATERIALS

Fabrics
Buttons
Thread to match
Pillow form(s)

TECHNIQUES

Read About Knife-Edge Pillows, pages 24–25. Refer to Part Three, Basics, for information on sewing techniques.

MEASURE, MARK, AND CUT

Note: Cut each button band to twice the desired finished depth. Add underlap allowances as indicated below. Add seam allowance to all edges of each section, including those with underlaps. Refer to the tip at the beginning of the directions for each sham before cutting the pieces.

End-Band Sham ✂ cut 1 of each piece

Ⓐ BUTTON BAND

Ⓑ SHAM FRONT ✂ subtract the button-band depth from the length

Ⓒ SHAM BACK ✂ add twice the button-band depth to the length for the fold-over underlap

Middle-Band Sham ✂ cut 1 of each piece

Ⓓ BUTTON BAND

Ⓔ BANDED SHAM FRONT ✂ subract the button-band depth from the length

Ⓕ SHAM BACK

Ⓖ UNDERLAPPED SHAM FRONT ✂ add twice the button-band depth to the length

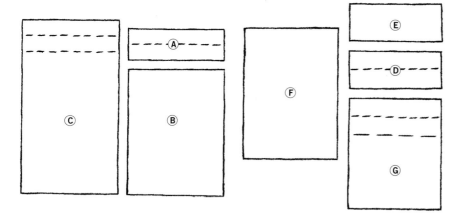

buttoned back-to-front shams

3 Fold the band in half again along the crease made in step 1, covering the seam allowance and lapping the finished edge over the seamline. Pin or baste. Stitch the band through all layers right next to the seamline. Referring to the photographs, mark and stitch buttonholes evenly spaced on the band. ▽

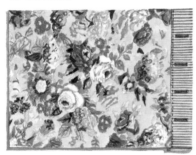

TIPS FROM THE PROS
✂Omit the side seam allowance when dividing the band for buttonholes.

4 Mark the fold-over button underlap on the sham back (C) as follows. Place the back right side up. With the cut edges aligned, place the sham front right side up on top of it. Using chalk, draw a line on the back along the folded edge of the band. Draw another line parallel to the first and the depth of the band away from it. Draw a third line this same distance from the second line. ▽

5 Remove the sham front. Turn the back wrong side up. Hem the marked end, folding the fabric to the wrong side along the middle line, and turning under (trim any excess fabric) or serging the end along the outer line; the inside edge of the hem should align with the inner marked line.

6 Place the back right side up. With the cut edges aligned, place the front right side down on top of it. Fold the extending hem over the button band. Pin along the cut edges. ▽

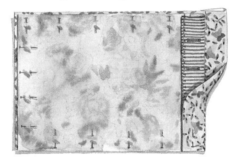

7 Sew the back to the front along the cut edges. Trim the seam allowance at the corners. Turn the sham right side out; the button underlap will fold against the wrong side of the back. Sew a button opposite each buttonhole. Insert the pillow form, tucking it into the pocket formed by the button underlap; fasten the buttons.

MIDDLE-BAND SHAM

TIPS FROM THE PROS
✂The easiest way to prepare this sham is to cut the fronts a little long and size them as explained in steps 2 and 3 below and right. This will enable you to shift the position of the band a bit to the right or left, if you wish.

1 Following steps 1–3 for the end-band sham, sew the button band (D) onto the appropriate sham front (E) and make the buttonholes. ▽

2 Place the sham back (F) on your worktable. With the cut ends aligned, place the underlapped sham front (G) on top of it right side up. With the opposite cut ends aligned, place the banded sham right side up on top of them. Using chalk, draw a line on the underlapped sham along the folded edge of the band. ▽

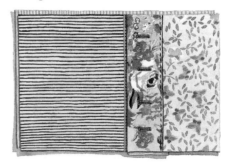

3 Remove the banded front. On the underlap, draw another line parallel to the first and the depth of the band away from it. Draw a third line this same distance from the second line. If the fabric extends more than $1/2$" beyond the last line, trim the excess. ▽

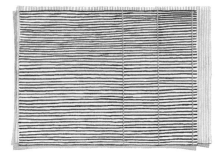

4 Remove the underlap and turn it wrong side up. Hem the marked end, folding the fabric to the wrong side along the middle line and turning under or serging the end along the outer line.

5 Place the back right side up. With the cut edges aligned, place first the banded front, then the hemmed front, wrong side up on top of it; the hem should overlap the band. Pin and sew the fronts to the back along the cut edges. ▷

6 Trim the seam allowance at the corners. Turn the sham right side out. Sew a button opposite each buttonhole. Insert the pillow form and fasten the buttons.

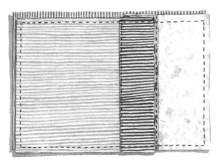

Use simple buttons with busy fabrics or let the buttons rule on a simpler background.

round sham

ABOUT THE SAMPLE

The sham is made from a lightweight cotton print with a glazed finish; it's trimmed with silk grosgrain ribbon. The sham is 13½" in diameter, including a ½"-deep self-flange that is concealed by the ruffle; it fits loosely on the pillow form.

MATERIALS

Fabric

Ribbon

Thread to match

Buttons or desired fastener for back closure

Pillow form

TECHNIQUES

Read About Knife-Edge Pillows, pages 24–25. Refer to Part Three, Basics, for information on overlap closures, calculating ruffle fullness, and other sewing techniques.

MEASURE, MARK, AND CUT

Note: Plan the finished sham to be 1½" larger in diameter than the pillow form. The ruffle is a tube. To find the cut depth of the ruffle strip, calculate its finished depth to include the header; double this dimension and add 1" (twice the seam allowance). Cut the sham back as a rectangle, including overlap and hem allowances in its width as shown; you'll cut it into a round later.

(A) **RUFFLE** ✂cut as many strips as needed

(B) **SHAM BACK** ✂cut 1

(C) **SHAM FRONT** ✂cut 1

1 Sew the pieces of the ruffle together to make one strip. Fold the strip in half lengthwise, wrong side out. Sew the long edges together to make a tube. ▽

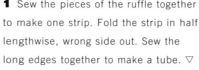

2 Press the seam allowance open. Turn the tube right side out. Center the seam on the underside of the tube and press the tube flat, creasing both long edges. ▽

3 On the side of the tube without the seam, sew grosgrain ribbon along one creased edge; sew both edges of the ribbon through both layers of the tube.

TIPS FROM THE PROS

✂When applying silk grosgrain ribbon by machine, use a very fine needle and two-ply cotton machine-embroidery thread; adjust the tension as needed.

4 Mark a line 1" (or the depth of your header) from and parallel to the opposite edge. Gather along the marked line (refer to Basics, page 114). ▽

5 To set up the overlap closure, cut the sham back (B) into two pieces (refer to page 117). Press the hem allowance to the wrong side of each piece along the overlap edge. Finish the inside edge of each hem, then stitch each hem.

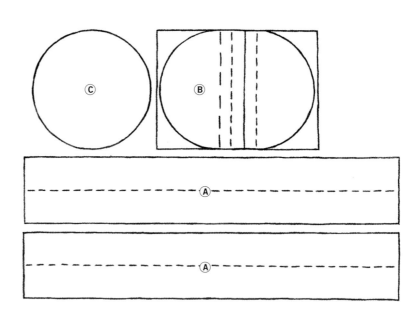

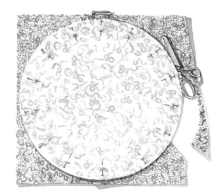

6 Place the sham backs right side up and overlap the hemmed edges; pin to hold temporarily. Center the sham front on the backs; pin. Trim the excess fabric from the sham back. △

7 Separate all the pieces. If desired, make buttonholes in the hem of one sham back (refer to page 121) or sew corresponding pieces of hook-and-loop tape to the inside of one hem and the outside of the other.

8 Place the sham backs right side up and overlap the hemmed edges; be sure the appropriate one is on top. Pin together at each end of the overlap. With the right sides together and cut edges aligned, pin the front to the back. Sew together around the perimeter.

9 Trim the seam allowance and turn the sham right side out through the overlap closure. Press the edge sharply.

A pretty ruffle topstitched onto a hidden flange does away with the waffling edges that often spoil round pillows. You could also use wide lace or ribbon for the ruffle— just avoid anything truly sheer.

10 On the right side of the sham front, mark a line 1/2" inside the perimeter. Pull up the gathering threads on the ruffle. Test the fit of the ruffle on the sham front, aligning the gathering stitches with the marked line and facing the header toward the center. Adjust the gathers so the ruffle fans nicely around the sham front. If it is too full, cut off the excess. ▽

11 Remove the ruffle and, using a French seam, sew the ends together (refer to Basics, page 114).

12 Reposition the ruffle on the sham front as before. Pin, then stitch along the gathering line. Center grosgrain ribbon over the stitching line, pin, and sew through all layers; overlap and finish the ribbon ends neatly.

13 If the sham back overlap has buttonholes, sew a button to the underlap opposite each. Insert the pillow form and fasten the closure.

ribbon-grid square

ABOUT THE SAMPLE

The pillow is raw silk with an appliquéd grid of sheer silk ribbon; small silk organza florets dot the center. Both sides of the sample are trimmed with the ribbon grid; if you prefer, you can make a plain back with an overlap closure (refer to Basics, page 117). The sample is 15" square.

MATERIALS

Fabric
Ribbon
Organza for florets
Thread to match
Pillow form

TECHNIQUES

Read About Knife-Edge Pillows, pages 24–25. Refer to Part Three, Basics, for information on sewing techniques.

MEASURE, MARK, AND CUT

Note: Cut the ribbon the same length as the pillow edge it will parallel (including seam allowance).

Ⓐ **PILLOW FRONT & BACK** ✂cut 2

Ⓑ **RIBBON** ✂cut 4 lengths each for the front and back

Ⓒ **FLORETS** ✂cut or tear 9, each 2" square

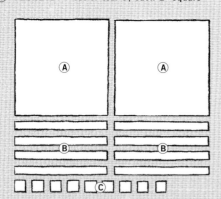

1 Using a ruler and chalk, mark the pillow front and back (A) for the ribbon appliqué. From each cut edge, measure in 3¹/₂" (or the desired distance from the cut edge to the outside edge of the ribbon). ▽

2 Aligning its outside edge with a marked line, pin ribbon (B) to two opposite edges of the front and of the back. Edgestitch the ribbon. ▽

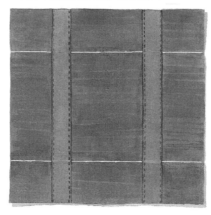

TIPS FROM THE PROS

✂To appliqué fine ribbon without creating puckers or pulls, put an edgestitch foot, if you have one, on your machine and sew with a fine (65/9) needle and two-ply machine-embroidery thread.

Silk organza is the ideal fabric to use for these informal floret twists—it doesn't fray badly, so you don't need to finish its edges, and because it's sheer, it both gives and takes color from the main fabric.

3 In the same way, sew ribbon parallel to the remaining edges of each piece. ▽

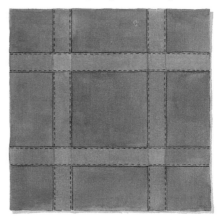

4 With right sides together and cut edges aligned, pin the front to the back. Sew them together, leaving an opening on one side. Trim the seam allowance at each corner. Press the seams open. Turn the pillow cover right side out.

5 Working as follows, make the florets and, placing them in three rows of three, sew them to one side of the pillow cover. ✂Fold two opposite edges of a torn organza square (C) to its center. ▽

✂Bringing the two remaining edges together, fold the organza in half. ▽

✂Thread a needle and knot the thread. Scrunch the fabric along the fold made in the last step and hold it together between your fingers as you take a stitch or two through it, wrap it a few times with thread, and stitch through it again to secure the wraps. ▽

TIPS FROM THE PROS
✂Don't cut the thread after wrapping the floret, sew it directly to your project.

6 Insert the pillow form and slipstitch the opening closed.

Tone-on-tone color and contrasting textures give a soft sophistication to this graphic design. Other options: Use boldly contrasting materials, trim the center with buttons or beads, or leave the grid unadorned.

about square-edge pillows

In this book, pillows that have distinct top, bottom, and side planes are grouped together. In some constructions side planes are formed when the corners of the top and bottom pieces of fabric are shaped with darts or gathers, which creates an informal, softly boxed shape. These are referred to as dart-shaped pillows. Pillows with a separate band of fabric between the top and bottom are referred to as boxed pillows.▽

DART-SHAPED PILLOW

BOXED PILLOW

No matter what size they are, square-edge pillows appear bulkier than their knife-edge counterparts. Boxed pillows in particular have a way of looking formal rather than casual when tossed on a piece of furniture, but the effect can be softened by your choice of fabric and filling. Rectangular dart-shaped pillows offer an informal alternative to bolsters; they'll sit comfortably inside the arm or against the back of a chair or sofa. And, unlike bolsters, their height is independent of their thickness.

MAKING DART-SHAPED PILLOWS

Dart-shaped pillows are made of two identical pieces of fabric that are sewn together around the edges; the seam falls on the sides, halfway between the top and bottom of the pillow. On pages 58–59 you'll find directions for making a basic dart-shaped pillow; follow them to make a pillow of any size. You can insert welting, a ruffle, or any trim desired in the seam, or leave it plain.

✂ If you'd prefer to make a pillow with a more formal shape, sew the darts closed; follow the directions for making a dart-shaped pillow form on page 112.

✂ Because the cover wraps onto the pillow sides, an overlap closure is inappropriate for this type of cover. If you wish to make the cover easily removable, insert a zipper in the seam on one edge; insert it before sewing the front to the back along the remaining three edges.

MAKING BOXED PILLOWS

To begin, decide the length, width, and thickness of your pillow. Boxed pillows should be filled with a form; loose stuffing won't hold a good shape unless stuffed very tightly, and then the pillow will be stiff. Although ready-made boxed pillow forms are not as widely available as are knife-edge ones, it's very easy to convert a knife-edge form to a mock-boxed shape—and certainly faster than it is to sew and stuff a form. If you'd like a firm pillow, consider using a foam form. Read About Pillow Forms in Basics, page 112.

TIPS FROM THE PROS
✂ Boxed pillows need not be square or rectangular. However, the more irregular the top and bottom shape, the more complex fitting and attaching the boxing will be. If the top and bottom are round, the pillow is really a bolster; turn to pages 72–73 for more information.

Planning the Fabric Placement
Before you make the pattern for the cover, give some thought to the way you plan to position the pieces on the fabric. The boxing strip can be cut with the long edge on either the lengthwise or crosswise grain. It is usually more economical to place it on the crosswise grain, but you might wish to take advantage of a fabric pattern such as a stripe, which could look attractive running around the pillow.

✂ Unless your pillow is very small, you'll probably have to piece the boxing if you cut it on the crosswise grain.

✂ To save fabric, piece boxing that is cut on the lengthwise grain.

✂ When using a napped fabric such as velvet, always cut the boxing on the crosswise grain.

Planning the Closure
The least obtrusive way to close a boxed pillow cover is by slipstitching the section of the seam left open so the form could be inserted. If you'd like your pillow cover to be easily removable, you have several options.

✂ Make the back with an overlap closure; refer to Basics, page 117.

✂ Close the cover with a zipper. Refer to Basics, pages 120–21, to see how to insert a zipper centered between the pillow top and bottom on the boxing or in a plain or welted seam.

Making a Cutting Pattern

The cover for a boxed pillow should be the same size as the form; a looser cover will look sloppy. If you'd like your pillow to look particularly plump or overstuffed, make the pattern a little bit smaller than the form.

✂For the front and back (or top and bottom) pattern, measure the top or bottom of the form and draft a pattern of the same dimensions.

✂For the boxing, measure the perimeter of the top/bottom pattern. If the total is greater than the width of your fabric, divide by 2. Measure the thickness of the pillow form. Draft a pattern with these dimensions.

✂Add ¹/₂" seam allowance all around both patterns.

TIPS FROM THE PROS

✂To conserve fabric or center a portion of the fabric design, it might be necessary to make a boxing pattern equal in length to each different side of the top/bottom. (If your pillow is rectangular rather than square, the sides won't all be the same length.)

✂Some people find it easier and more accurate to cut the boxing strips a bit longer than necessary, sew them individually to the pillow top/front and then seam their ends together and trim off the excess.

Sewing the Cover

On both long edges of the boxing, measure and mark the length of the seamline (not the cut edge) of each edge of the pillow top. Be sure to allow seam allowance at the ends of the boxing strip and mark the pillow edges in consecutive order if they are not all the same length.

With the right sides together and cut edges aligned, sew the ends of the boxing strips together to form a ring; leave ¹/₂" open at each end of the seam. ▽

Positioning the boxing seam(s) and marks at the corners, pin the boxing to the pillow top; at each corner, clip the seam allowance of the boxing up to the seamline to enable it to pivot; refer to Basics, page 116. Sew the boxing to the pillow top. ▽

Repeat to sew the boxing to the pillow bottom, sewing around four corners and three sides and leaving most of the fourth side open so you can insert the pillow form.

Trim the seam allowance at each corner. You can press the seams open onto the boxing or onto the top and bottom, whichever seems to best distribute their bulk. Turn the cover right side out, insert the pillow form, and slipstitch the opening closed.

TIPS FROM THE PROS

✂If you wish, you can sew the boxing to the pillow without joining the ends or pinning it first. Align the long edge of the boxing with one side of the pillow top and place the pieces in the machine with the boxing on top. Sew the first side exactly up to the next corner seamline (¹/₂" from the adjacent edge), stopping with the needle down. Lift the presser foot, clip the boxing seam allowance up to the seamline, pivot both pieces, align the cut edges as before, and repeat until the boxing is sewn to all four sides of the top. Then sew the ends of the boxing together.

✂There's really nothing wrong with placing the seam joining the boxing along one side of the pillow. It might be more apparent, but there will be less stress on it. This placement can be helpful when working with fragile fabrics or, oddly enough, if you want to minimize the bulk of heavier ones.

DESIGN IDEAS

Let the pillow top show off a wonderful or unique piece of fabric—perhaps something you created or found, such as a quilt square, a piece of embroidery, or a hand-painted textile.

Dress up or change the character of the pillow by inserting trim in the perimeter seams before attaching the boxing. Welting is the traditional choice, but fringe and ruffles can also be used. Keep an eye on the proportions of any trims; a deep ruffle will overwhelm the boxing and look silly, while a shallow one can be witty. Because you add trim while the cover pieces are flat, you attach it the same way you do on a knife-edge pillow; turn to page 25 for more information.

softly boxed pillow

ABOUT THE SAMPLE

The sample is made from two flat rectangles of print fabric. There is a double layer of cut fringe inserted in the seam. Read the tip at right before cutting your pillow cover.

This pillow is not truly a square-edge pillow; it gets its boxy shape from loose darts folded at each corner. The sample is 14" from top to bottom and 18" from side to side measured across the center. To determine what size to make yours, bear in mind that the thickness of the pillow will be subtracted from its length and width once it is stuffed. Before cutting your fabric, read the directions for preparing the pillow form.

MATERIALS

Fabric
Fringe
Thread to match
Pillow form

TECHNIQUES

Read About Square-Edge Pillows, pages 56–57. Refer to Part Three, Basics, for information on sewing techniques.

MEASURE, MARK, AND CUT

Note: Measure lengthwise and widthwise around your pillow form; divide each dimension in half. To each, add twice the seam allowance. Cut the pillow cover pieces to the last dimensions.

Ⓐ **PILLOW COVER FRONT & BACK** ✀cut 2

TIPS FROM THE PROS

✀Pillows made in this fashion look best if the covers sit loosely over their forms. So plan yours to be a little larger than your form; you can add loose stuffing to fill out the corners if you decide they look too casual.

PILLOW FORM

✀If you wish to use a foam form, wrap it in batting to soften its edges.
✀If you wish to use a soft ready-made form, use one with knife edges and follow the directions on page 112 for making a mock-boxed pillow.
✀If you wish to make a soft form, follow the directions below, omitting the fringe.

COVER

1 To find the length to make the corner darts, measure the thickness of your pillow form; divide this dimension in half. For example, if your pillow form is 3" thick, the corner dart will be $1\frac{1}{2}$" long.

Ⓐ

2 Place the pillow cover front and back (A) wrong side up. At each corner, mark the seam allowance along the edges. From each marked corner, measure and mark the length of the dart on each seamline. ▽

3 At each corner fold the fabric diagonally, wrong side out, aligning the adjacent cut edges (fold along the dash line in the drawing above). Perpendicular to the cut edge, place a pin through the mark made in the last step. ▽

4 Keeping the fabric wrong side out, slide your fingers between the layers to open one boxed corner. Flatten and center the dart over the pinned corner; pin as shown, keeping the pin heads below the cut side edges. Repeat at each corner. ▽

5 Remove the pins inserted in step 3. From the right side, trim the points of fabric extending above the cut side edges. Baste across the end of each dart to secure it.

6 Place the cover front right side up. Pin the fringe to it, aligning the edge of the header tape with the cut edge of the fabric; begin and end on one side and finish the fringe ends neatly. Sew the fringe to the fabric. ▽

A double layer of short cotton fringe adds a plump, plush finish to this vibrant cotton print.

TIPS FROM THE PROS

✂To prevent the corners from collapsing upon themselves when you sew the front to the back in the next step, narrow the seam allowance at each corner by shifting the fringe tape out and off the fabric about $1/4$".

✂To achieve a luxurious finish, use two layers of fringe. Apply one continuous strip, wrapping it twice around the perimeter.

7 With the right sides together and cut edges aligned, pin the front to the back. Sew them together, leaving an opening on one side.

A rectangular softly boxed pillow can stand in for a bolster; here fringe defines its silhouette. The ruffled pillow is a basic knife-edge design; see page 26. To make the fold-over pillow slip, see pages 38–39.

8 Turn the pillow cover right side out. Insert the pillow form and slipstitch the opening closed.

TIPS FROM THE PROS

✂Cover the fringe loosely with masking or transparent tape so you don't sew it while you're slipstitching.

serpentine-
ruched sham

ABOUT THE SAMPLE

The sample is made from two flat pieces of damask. The serpentine ruche is made of 1½"-wide wire-edged ribbon; you'll need a length of ribbon equal to about five times the perimeter of the pillow form plus 12" for each rosette.

This pillow is not truly a square-edge pillow; it gets its plump shape from gathers sewn at each corner. The sample measures 18" from side to side across the center. To determine what size to make yours, bear in mind that the thickness of the pillow will be subtracted from its length and width once it is stuffed. Before cutting your fabric, read the pillow form directions.

MATERIALS

Fabric
Ribbon
Button forms to cover
Desired fastener for back closure
Thread to match
Pillow form

TECHNIQUES

Read About Square-Edge Pillows, pages 56–57. Refer to Part Three, Basics, for information on overlap closures and other sewing techniques.

MEASURE, MARK, AND CUT

Note: Measure lengthwise and widthwise around your pillow form; divide each dimension in half. To each, add twice the seam allowance. Cut the sham front to the last dimensions. Cut the back wider to allow for the overlap closure.

Ⓐ **SHAM BACK** ✂cut 1
Ⓑ **SHAM FRONT** ✂cut 1

PILLOW FORM

✂If you wish to use a ready-made form, use a soft one with knife edges. Push the filling away from each corner, gather on a curved line inside the corner (refer to step 2 below), trim the excess fabric, and hand stitch the gathered seam allowance to one side of the form.

✂If you wish to make a form, cut two identical pieces of fabric, follow steps 2 and 3 below, leaving an opening on one edge so you can turn the cover right side out. Stuff the cover and slipstitch the opening closed.

SHAM

1 Make the overlap closure on the sham back (A), trimming the back to the same size as the front, applying the fastening, and pinning the overlap closed at the hem ends (refer to Basics, page 117).

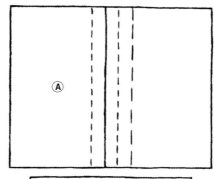

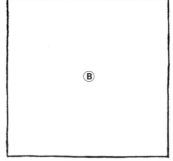

2 On the right side of the fabric, mark a curved line at each corner of the sham front (B) and back; begin and end on the seamline about 3" from the corner. By machine, sew gathering stitches along both sides of each line. Place a pin at one end of each pair of gathering stitches and wrap the threads around it. Pull the threads at the opposite end and distribute the fullness evenly along them; wrap them around another pin. Trim the fabric at each corner, ½" from the marked line. ▽

3 With the right sides together and cut edges aligned, pin and sew the front to the back. Press the seam open. Turn the sham right side out.

4 Referring to the Designer Detail, page 62, make a length of ribbon ruching for each edge of the sham; make the ruches long enough to overlap at the sham corners.

TIPS FROM THE PROS

✂You might be tempted to make one length of ruching to go all the way around the pillow. Unless you're making a very small pillow, you'll find it easier to handle a separate piece for each edge.

5 Centering the ruche over the seamline, pin the midpoint of each ruche to the midpoint of one edge of the sham, then pin toward each corner. Using a stab stitch (refer to Basics, page 113), sew each ruche to the sham. ▽

A pretty moiré ribbon combines with elegant damask to make a dressy throw pillow. Use grosgrain for a sportier interpretation, as seen on the cover.

TIPS FROM THE PROS

✄ If the ribbon has an ombré or other variegated pattern, be sure to orient like edges in the same direction.

✄ You'll probably find it easier to sew on the ruche if you place one hand inside the sham.

6 At each corner, turn under the overlapping end of the ruche and slipstitch to the adjacent piece. If you have to trim any excess length, don't cut through the gathering stitches— pull them out and reknot to maintain their tension.

7 Cover four buttons with the ribbon.

8 Make four ribbon rosettes. For each, cut a 12" length of ribbon. Sew hand-gathering stitches along one edge. Pull up the gathers to create a ring and knot or tie the threads together. Sew the ends of the ribbon together neatly by hand. ▷

9 Sew a rosette to each corner of the sham. Sew a covered button in the center of each rosette. Insert the pillow form and fasten the closure.

serpentine ruching

This ruche is hand gathered in a soft zigzag pattern; when the gathers are drawn up, scallops form on both edges. You can make this kind of ruche from ribbon, with or without a wire edge. You can also use a tube of fabric or a strip with finished edges.

TIPS FROM THE PROS

✂ The width and hand of your ribbon affect the look of the ruche. Experiment to find the best proportion and tension of the gathering stitches.

✂ Loosely woven or poor quality ribbons may not hold up to the stress of the gathers. Buy a small length and experiment before purchasing the total yardage.

1 Using a ruler and chalk, mark parallel lines 2" apart across the ribbon. ▽

2 Using the chalk lines to guide alternate high and low points, sew short running stitches in a curved zigzag pattern over the entire ribbon length. ▽

3 Slide the ribbon along the gathering stitches to create an evenly scalloped ruche.

✂ Place a pin at each end and wrap the thread around it so you can adjust the tension further when you apply the ruche to your project.

✂ When the ruche is almost completely stitched to the project, knot the gathering thread or secure it with a few stitches.

TIPS FROM THE PROS

✂ If possible, use one length of thread for each ruche so you won't have to work around knots when you are adjusting the ruche on your project. Work with a manageable length and slide the fabric along the stitches as you sew. If you must add a second length of thread, keep plenty of excess at each end so the fabric doesn't slide off when you adjust the tension.

✂ Use polyester thread to minimize breakage. Use a milliner's (extralong) needle so you can sew more stitches at one time.

The color of this ribbon fades from dark to light to create an ombré, or shadow, effect. The wire edge helps the ruche to keep its scallop shape, but isn't necessary. You can also make a ruche from a strip of bias-cut fabric—the bias won't ravel; tafetta is an ideal choice. For more interest, try pinking the edges.

TIPS FROM THE PROS

✂If you arrange the ribbons on a cork board or other surface into which you can pin, it will be easy to adjust the spacing after you've woven them.

✂For extra stability, use a fusible fabric for the lining. Place it fusible side up, weave the ribbons, and baste as described on the next page, then fuse. If using velvet ribbon, be sure to turn the woven top over, place it on a velvet board, and press from the wrong side.

A woven checkerboard of wide velvet ribbons trimmed with small beads makes a handsome pillow top. Because velvet reflects light, you can create some interesting effects by using subtly contrasting colors; try a single color for understated elegance.

ABOUT THE SAMPLE

The pillow top and sides are made of $3^1/8$"-wide velvet ribbon; the back is velveteen. The pillow is about 16" square. The woven top is mounted on a coordinating lining; at each interstice a glass seed bead is sewn through a glass pony bead to the lining. To create a checkerboard with symmetrical corners, you must use an odd number of ribbon bands in each direction; there are five bands on the sample.

MATERIALS

Lining
Ribbon, two colors or as desired
Velveteen or other backing fabric
Seed and pony beads
Desired fastener for back closure
Thread to match
Pillow form

TECHNIQUES

Read About Square-Edge Pillows, pages 56–57. Refer to Part Three, Basics, for information on overlap closures and other sewing techniques.

MEASURE, MARK, AND CUT

Note: The width of the ribbon and number of bands used in each direction will dictate the size of your pillow. Purchase sufficient ribbon in one of the colors to make the boxing as well as the top. Cut the back after weaving the top, making it wide enough to allow for an overlap closure.

Ⓐ **PILLOW TOP LINING** ✂cut 1, trim to final size after weaving the pillow top

Ⓑ **RIBBON BANDS** ✂cut each length 1½" longer than desired finished dimension

Ⓒ **PILLOW BACK** ✂cut 1

Ⓓ **BOXING** ✂use ribbon or fabric, as you wish

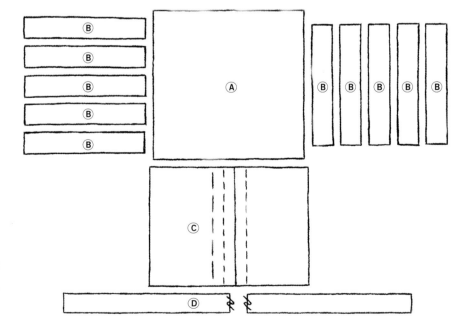

woven-ribbon square

1 Place the lining (A) right side up on your work surface. Center and lay five bands (B) of the same color ribbon vertically, side by side, on the lining so their sides are not quite touching. Pin the ribbons to the work surface through the lining. ▽

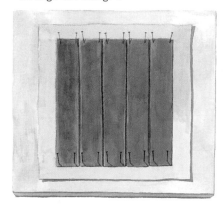

2 From the other color ribbon, weave five bands horizontally through the bands pinned to the lining. Use a simple basket-weave pattern, passing the first band alternately under, then over, the vertical bands, and the next band over, then under them. You'll find it easier to weave the ribbon if you attach a small metal bodkin (or a safety pin) to the leading end. ▽

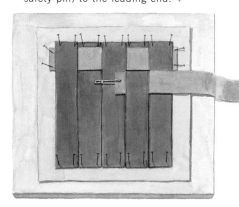

3 Continue in the same manner to weave the three remaining bands. Working from the center out, adjust the ribbon so it lies smoothly over the lining; keep the horizontal and vertical ribbons perpendicular to one another and parallel to the lining edges. Pin the ribbons to the lining at the perimeter.

TIPS FROM THE PROS

✂The thickness of the ribbon affects the overall size of the woven area. Velvet ribbon will weave into a slightly larger area than will satin or grosgrain.
✂The bands should fit closely together at the woven interstices but their edges might not butt at the perimeter—don't force them; the finished pillow will pucker if you do.

4 Sewing through all three layers, baste the ribbons to the lining around the perimeter. Be sure to sew through the edge of the ribbon where it's hidden by the top layer of the woven pattern. △

TIPS FROM THE PROS

✂Don't skip the basting step, even if you fuse the ribbon to the lining. The ends of the top layer of ribbon must be secured before you sew the pillow top to the boxing.

5 Trim the lining and ribbon ends $1/2$" from the basting to create a seam allowance. If necessary, finish the edges of the pillow top to keep the ribbon and lining from fraying.

6 Measure the pillow top and cut the back (C) to the appropriate dimensions, allowing for an overlap closure. Make the overlap closure, trimming the back to the same size as the front, applying the fastening, and pinning the overlap closed at the hem ends (refer to page 117).

7 Measure the perimeter of the pillow top, add 1" for seam allowance, and cut a length of ribbon to this dimension for the boxing (D). (If you're making the boxing from fabric, add seam allowance on each edge.)

8 With the right sides together and beginning at the middle of one side of the top, pin the boxing to the top. Align the edge of the boxing ribbon with the edge of the ribbon on the pillow top, and pin just inside them. ▽

9 Continue to pin, pivoting the boxing around each corner in a slight curve. When you reach the starting point, pin the ends of the boxing together, but don't sew at this time.

10 Sew the boxing to the pillow top, stitching just inside the edge of the ribbon. Then sew the seam joining the ends of the boxing.

TIPS FROM THE PROS

✂ Velvet ribbon tends to shift and stretch under the presser foot. Baste first or, better yet, sew the boxing on by hand with a small backstitch.

11 Sew beads to the interstices of the weave. Bring the needle up from the wrong side of the lining, between the ribbons, passing it through a pony bead, then through a seed bead; pass it back through the pony bead and lining. Pull the thread taut, nesting the seed bead in the hole of the pony bead. Knot and cut the thread. Repeat.

12 Mark the seamline on the wrong side of the back. With the right sides together, pin the boxing to the back; place the boxing seam on an edge without overlapping hem ends. Sew the boxing to the back.

13 Turn the pillow cover right side out and insert the pillow form.

Look for beads or buttons that suit your ribbon—glass, plastic, metal, wood, even passementerie are some options. Directions for the wrapped bolster are on pages 82–83.

knotted-
corner pillow

ABOUT THE SAMPLE

The sample is made from two lightweight cotton batiks. The flat cover is tied over a 20"-square boxed pillow form. The weight of your fabric will affect the look and fit of the knotted corners, so read the directions and test-fit a sample corner on your form before cutting your cover. If you use two fabrics, they should be the same weight.

MATERIALS

Fabric(s)
Thread to match
Pillow form

TECHNIQUES

Read About Square-Edge Pillows, pages 56–57. Refer to Part Three, Basics, for information on sewing techniques.

MEASURE, MARK, AND CUT

Note: Refer to steps 1 and 2 of the directions to make a pattern for your pillow cover and figure the amount of fabric you'll need.

(A) PILLOW COVER FRONT & BACK ✂cut 2
(1 from each fabric)

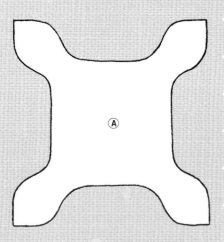

1 Draft a quarter pattern on a piece of paper: Measure and add together the width and thickness of your pillow form; add 1¹/₂" for ease and seam allowance. Divide this number in half and draw a square that size. Draw a diagonal line from corner to corner in one direction, extending the line about 9" beyond one corner. Draw a wide lozenge shape as shown, making it about 8" at the widest point. ▽

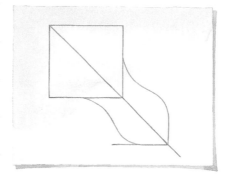

TIPS FROM THE PROS

✂Be sure your lozenge shape is symmetrical. Fold the pattern along the diagonal line and, using a needle-point wheel, trace the shape through both layers, then redraw the outline along the perforations.

✂You can have a lot of fun with the corners for this pillow. Try making them longer, rounded, scalloped; split each into two or more sections; or exaggerate them in some other way. Alternatively, make them very short so each creates a perky frill just below the knot.

✂Think about the pattern on your fabric before cutting the cover. If you are using a plaid or check, it might be fun cut on the bias. Cut your test sample on the bias to be sure the knot ties attractively.

Batiks seem a natural choice for this saronglike design, where knotted lozenge-shape corners add a casual flourish, but this pillow cover is cleverly contoured to permit almost any weight fabric to knot gracefully.

2 Extend the outline of the square from a nonlozenge corner. As shown by the arrow, measure from the tip of the lozenge to this line; double the number. You need a square of fabric this size for each piece of the pillow cover (A). ▽

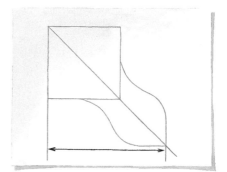

3 Cut out the pattern. Fold one piece of your fabric in half lengthwise, then widthwise, to quarter it. Place the pattern on it, positioning the corner opposite the lozenge at the folded corner as shown. △

4 Draw around the pattern, remove it, and cut out the fabric. Repeat with the other piece of fabric.

5 Unfold the fabrics and place them right sides together, aligning the cut edges; pin. Using a ¹/₂" seam allowance, sew them together; leave one side open between the lozenges. Clip and trim the seam allowance around the lozenge as necessary for your fabric. ▽

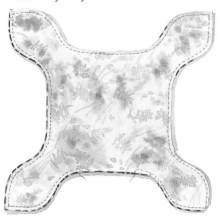

6 Press the straight portions of the seam open. Turn the cover right side out. Press the seamed edge of each lozenge sharply. Insert the pillow form and slipstitch the opening closed.

7 Tie each corner in a loose knot. ▽

TIPS FROM THE PROS
✄ Twist the corners so they match or contrast the adjacent side of the pillow cover, as you wish.

For a more sophisticated look, try this design in a changeable silk or a soft velvet; add lightweight trim to the perimeter seam or wrap the knot with cording and tassels. Or, appliqué a decorative medallion in the middle of the front before sewing the pieces together.

mock-welted
padded sham

ABOUT THE SAMPLE

The cover for this boxed pillow is cut larger than the form, backed with batting, sewn together, and then hand stitched along the seamlines to create "welting." The sample is made of lightweight denim, the pillow form is 20" square and 4" high, the finished cover is 22" square and 6" high, with 1"-wide "welting" stitched along each seam. Different fabrics and sizes will result in different effects.

MATERIALS

Fabric

Batting

Muslin lining

Desired fastener for back closure

Pearl cotton or other decorative thread for hand stitching

Thread to match

Pillow form

TECHNIQUES

Read About Square-Edge Pillows, pages 56–57. Refer to Part Three, Basics, for information on overlap closures and other sewing techniques.

MEASURE, MARK, AND CUT

Note: Measure your pillow form, add twice the desired thickness of the "welt" to each dimension of the front and back and to the height of the boxing, then add seam allowance to all pieces; cut the sham back wide enough to allow for an overlap closure. For each piece, cut an identical piece of batting and lining.

(A) **SHAM TOP** ✂cut 1

(B) **SHAM BOTTOM** ✂cut 1

(C) **BOXING** ✂cut as many strips as needed

1 Place the sham top (A) wrong side up and top with a piece of batting, then with a piece of lining. Pin the layers together and baste along the seamlines. ▽

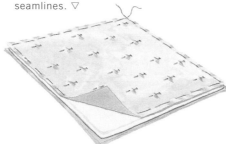

2 In the same manner, baste batting and lining to the boxing strips. Sew the ends of the boxing strips together to form a ring.

3 To set up the overlap closure, cut the sham bottom (B) into two pieces (refer to Basics, page 117). Press the hem allowance to the wrong side of each piece along the overlap edge.

This boxed pillow only looks as though it's trimmed with matching welting. The cover is padded with batting, and hand stitches pinch a ridge along the seams.

4 Place the sham bottoms wrong side up and unfold the hem allowance. Top each piece with a piece of batting, then with a piece of lining; align the batting and lining with the foldline of the hem allowances. Pin the layers together, trim the batting and lining even with the outer edges of the bottoms, and baste together along the seamlines. ▽

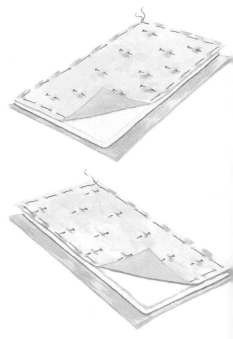

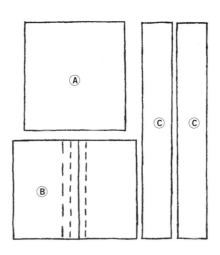

5 Pin the hems over the linings and topstitch to secure. If desired, make buttonholes in the hem of one bottom (refer to page 121); or sew corresponding pieces of hook-and-loop tape to the inside of one hem and the outside of the other.

6 Overlap the hems and trim the sham bottom to the same size as the sham top (refer to Basics, page 117).

7 With the right sides together and cut edges aligned, pin and sew the boxing to the sham top and bottom. Do not trim the batting from the seam allowance. Turn the sham right side out.

8 Pin the top and boxing together 1" inside the seamline; ease the boxing onto the top at each corner. Using pearl cotton, sew them together by hand with long running stitches. Repeat to hand sew the bottom to the boxing. ▽

9 If the overlap has buttonholes, sew a button to the underlap opposite each. Insert the pillow form and fasten the closure.

Soft fabrics and a soft form make this pillow inviting. Because they're padded, the cover top or boxing could easily be quilted in a simple decorative pattern. Directions for the round pillow begin on page 46.

ruched-boxing square

ABOUT THE SAMPLE

The sides of this basic boxed pillow feature a ruched (gathered) strip of metallic organza laid over a flat strip of velvet; the welting is also layered; the top and bottom are velvet only. The sample is 18" square, with 4"-deep boxing.

MATERIALS

Fabrics

Cable cord for welting

Thread to match

Pillow form

TECHNIQUES

Read About Square-Edge Pillows, pages 56–57. Refer to Part Three, Basics, for information on sewing techniques. If you wish to make the pillow cover removable, read about overlap closures on page 117; however, an overlap closure is not recommended when the fabric layers are bulky.

MEASURE, MARK, AND CUT

Note: The fullness of the ruching shown is 2½ times the perimeter of the pillow. If making an overlap closure, cut the pillow backs sufficiently wide to allow for the hems.

Ⓐ **BIAS STRIPS FOR WELTING** ✂cut 1¾" wide, sufficient to rim pillow top and bottom; cut equal amounts from velvet and organza

Ⓑ **PILLOW TOP & BOTTOM** ✂cut 2

Ⓒ **BOXING UNDERLAYER** ✂cut as many strips as needed

Ⓓ **RUCHING** ✂cut as many strips as needed to achieve desired fullness

1 Make the welting (A). With the right sides together and cut edges aligned, sew welting around the perimeter of the pillow top (B) and pillow bottom (B); overlap the ends on a side, not at a corner, and finish them neatly. (Refer to Basics, pages 118–19.) ▽

TIPS FROM THE PROS

✂Pile and flat woven fabrics behave differently. For best results when making the sheer-over-velvet welting, first piece the layers separately, then hand baste them together along both long edges.

✂Experiment to find the best presser foot to use for sewing the welting. Try a walking or even-feed foot, a Teflon-coated foot, or a roller foot. You might also wish to adjust the head tension (the pressure on the foot) if applicable to your machine.

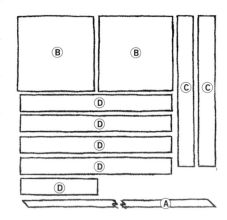

Although metallic organza has crossed the line from apparel to home furnishings, most vendors stock it with the eveningwear fabrics rather than with the chintzes.

2 Sew the pieces of the boxing underlayer (C) together to make one strip. Test the fit of the boxing by pinning the underlayer to the pillow top or by measuring, and mark the seamline for joining the underlayer ends. Cut off the excess fabric; be sure to leave seam allowance at each end.

3 Sew the pieces of the ruching (D) together to make one strip. Sew gathering stitches on both long edges; use a zigzag stitch over a strand of heavy thread so the stitches will adjust easily without breaking. Pull up the gathers. (Refer to Basics, page 114.)

4 Place the boxing underlayer right side up. Place the ruching right side up on top of it. Align the cut edges at one end and pin together. Wrap the gathering threads around the pins to secure them temporarily and adjust the ruching until it fits as desired on the underlayer. ▽

5 Beginning and ending a couple of inches from each end, hand baste the edges of the ruching to the underlayer. Cut off any excess ruching even with the ends of the underlayer.

TIPS FROM THE PROS

✂Pull the end of heavy thread from under the zigzag stitches on the excess ruching before cutting—if you cut through the heavy thread, you'll lose the gathers.

6 Remove the pins holding the ruching to the ends of the underlayer. Sew the ends of the ruching together. ▽

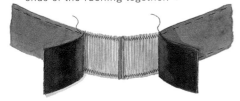

7 Sew the ends of the underlayer together. Press the seam allowance of both layers open with your fingers and finish basting the edges of the ruching to the underlayer.

8 With the right sides together and cut edges aligned, pin and sew the boxing to the pillow top; clip and pivot the boxing at each corner (refer to Basics, page 116). Leaving an opening on one side, pin and sew the boxing to the pillow bottom. Trim the corners, turn the cover right side out, insert the pillow form, and slipstitch the opening closed.

To make this ruched boxing, you can begin with crystal-pleated organza, as we did, or flat organza; in either case, gather both long edges onto a flat backing strip. Of course, all sorts of fabrics can be used—the possible effects are myriad.

about bolsters and rounds

Bolsters are traditionally used to soften the space between the seat and arms of a formal sofa, to provide support along the ends or back of a daybed, or as neckroll pillows on a bed. Changing the relative proportions of the diameter and length of a bolster can produce some interesting pillows, so don't limit your perception of these stalwarts. Of course, the larger you make a bolster, the more cumbersome it will be; the longer it is in proportion to its diameter, the more flexible—or floppy—the finished piece.

A cylindrical bolster cover can be as simple as an open tube of fabric with the ends tied or drawn closed, or more structured, with the ends of the tube enclosed with sewn-on rounds. ▽

**COVER WITH
DRAWSTRING ENDS**

**COVER WITH
SEWN-ON ENDS**

Of course, bolsters need not be cylindrical; you'll find a few in this book that are not. Before making them, read as well About Square-Edge Pillows, pages 56–57.

TIPS FROM THE PROS
✂When a bolster is very short, the ends become more important than the sides. Short bolsters make great round pillows.

GETTING STARTED
To begin, decide the size and proportion of the bolster. Many people find it difficult to visualize the effect of a bolster from a mathematical proportion, so don't hesitate to make or purchase a form and test it "on location" before you make the cover. As with any pillow, the type of form used influences the finished effect; somehow this is more pronounced for a bolster. Note that foam forms, with their perfectly flat ends and unforgiving sides, appear especially rigid. If you'd like the ends to be slightly domed, use a form with loose stuffing; if the cover has sewn-on ends, you can omit the form if you wish and stuff the cover directly.

Measuring for a Bolster Cover
To plan the size of a bolster cover, you need to know the length, circumference, and diameter of the form. Depending upon the type of cover you're making, you'll use these measurements in different ways. If you've forgotten the geometry of a circle, there is a math review on page 110. ▽

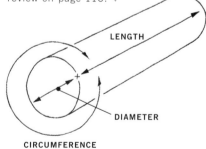

LENGTH

DIAMETER

CIRCUMFERENCE

Generally, covers with rounds sewn onto the ends look best if they fit closely; if they are too loose the ends will look sloppy. On the other hand, the fit of an open-end cover is a matter of the effect desired. To determine the fit, measure the circumference of the form and add ease as you wish.

MAKING AN OPEN-END COVER
Open-end covers are extremely easy to make. The simplest is just a tube tied or knotted at each end; all it requires is one lengthwise seam and two hems. The pillow on pages 80–81 is based on this construction.

To figure the size to cut a simple tube cover, measure and add together the length and the diameter of the form. To this measurement, add twice the amount you'd like to extend beyond the ends, considering whether this excess will be wrapped and tied with a cord or knotted over itself. On your fabric, draft a rectangle; make one dimension equal to the bolster circumference plus seam allowance, the other equal to your total length calculation plus hem allowance.

To make the cover, cut out the marked rectangle. Sew the lengthwise seam and press it open. Hem each end. Slide the cover over the form, centering it so the ends extend evenly, and tie as planned.

MAKING A DRAWSTRING-END COVER
Covers with drawstring ends are also very easy to sew, but determining the length to cut the cover requires precise planning. The drawstring closure on a bolster leaves a small circular opening on each end. The size of this opening is dictated by the weight of the fabric—the heavier the fabric, the less tightly it will be condensed by the drawstring and the larger the opening will be. The diameter of the opening should be subtracted when you calculate the overall length of the cover. The only way you can really know the size of this opening is to make a sample in your fabric.

1 Measure the circumference of your bolster; add twice the seam allowance. Cut a strip of your fabric this wide and 6"–8" deep (or at least the radius of the bolster plus 3").

2 Determine the depth needed to make the casing (the width of the drawstring plus ¹/8", but at least ¹/2"). On the right side of the fabric strip, mark a line ¹/2" from one long edge. Mark a second line parallel to and the casing depth away from the first line. ▽

3 At the ends of the strip, transfer the lines to the wrong side of the fabric. Sew the ends together, leaving the seam open between the marked lines. Press the seam open.

4 Fold the fabric to the wrong side along the second marked line and press the crease. Stitch through both layers along the first marked line. ▽

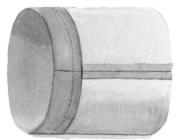

5 Feed the drawstring through the casing (use a safety pin or bodkin as a guide). Draw up the fabric as tightly as can be easily done and secure by tying together the drawstring ends.

6 Fan the fabric into a ring. Center it over the end of your bolster and smooth onto the side to be sure it is big enough around. Measure the diameter of the opening inside the drawstring. ▽

7 To determine the length to cut your bolster cover, measure and add together the length and diameter of the bolster. To allow for a casing on each end, add twice the allowance determined in step 2. To compensate for the gap inside the drawn-up fabric at each end, subtract the diameter of the opening once (thus subtracting the radius of the opening from each end).

8 Cut out the cover. Sew the lengthwise seam. Mark and sew a casing at each end as you did for your sample.

TIPS FROM THE PROS

✂If you don't plan ahead, you'll find it impossible to center any fabric pattern on your bolster. Don't skip the sample step unless your fabric is plain or has only a lengthwise stripe, in which case you can cut the cover extra long, put the casing in one end, fit the cover and then put the casing in the other end.
✂If the circular opening inside the drawstring is too large to be pleasing, you can cover it with a button or tuck a scrap of fabric inside it. Or you can trim it with a rosette, as shown on page 76.

MAKING A CLOSED-END COVER

There are a couple of tricks to making a bolster cover with closed, sewn-on round ends, and once you know them, the process is easy. The first is to plan to insert the bolster form through an opening in the side seam, not through one end. The second is to staystitch the end seamlines before sewing the pieces together.

To begin, measure the bolster form and cut two circles the diameter of the form plus seam allowance and one rectangle the length by the circumference of the form plus seam allowances. Press under the seam allowance on the long edges of the rectangle and staystitch the seamline on each end. Staystitch the seamline of each circle.

TIPS FROM THE PROS

✂To dress up this basic design, stitch welting around the perimeter of each circle; align the edge of the welting flange with the cut edge of the circle.

With the right sides together, pin and sew each end of the rectangle to the edge of a circle; clip the rectangle seam allowance so it follows the curve. ▽

Trim the seam allowance. Turn the cover right side out, insert the form, and slipstitch the opening closed.

tuck-trimmed bolster

ABOUT THE SAMPLE

The bolster cover is a one-piece tube of printed cotton chintz with drawstring closures; the flange at each end is a tuck folded and stitched in the tube. The tucks are trimmed with soutache. The bolster shown is 17" long and 8½" in diameter; the tucks are 1½" deep.

MATERIALS

Fabric
Soutache for trim and drawstring
Thread to match
Pillow form

TECHNIQUES

Read About Bolsters and Rounds, pages 72–73. Refer to Part Three, Basics, for information on sewing techniques.

MEASURE, MARK, AND CUT

Note: Plan the size of the cover as explained on pages 72–73, and add 6" for two 1½"-deep tucks. Measure the circumference of the bolster and add twice the seam allowance. Cut the cover to these dimensions.

Ⓐ **BOLSTER COVER** ✂cut 1

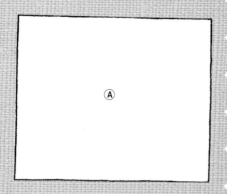

1 Place the cover (A) right side up. Measure the length of the bolster. Center and mark this dimension on both long edges of the cover. Using a nonpermanent fabric marker, draw lines across the fabric to connect the marks. Parallel to each line and 1½" closer to each end, draw another line. Also draw lines at each end for the casing as you did to make your drawstring fit test. ▽

TIPS FROM THE PROS

✂The bolster in the photo has a very narrow trim, which can be sewn on after the tucks are stitched. If you wish to use a wider trim, position it on the body of the bolster, inside the tuck, and sew it on now.

2 With the wrong side out, fold the cover in half lengthwise. Sew the long edges together, leaving the seam open at each end between the marked lines; backstitch on each side of each opening to reinforce the seam for the drawstring. ▽

Tucks folded into this one-piece cover create a flange at each end of the bolster. Add trim to the tucks where they're stitched, as shown, or along the inside or outside of the fold, or in both places.

3 Finish all the cut edges. Press the seam open. At each end fold the casing allowance to the wrong side and stitch through both layers on the marked line.

4 Turn the cover right side out. To form a tuck at each end, fold the fabric to the inside along the outer marked line and pin through both layers on the inner line. Sew the tucks where pinned. △

TIPS FROM THE PROS

✄ If you have a free arm on your machine, slip the cover over it and sew from the outside.

✄ If you do not have a free arm, turn the cover wrong side out and sew around the inside of the tube.

Use this design for a neckroll pillow or make it in another fabrication for a sofa; it would also look great as a daybed bolster.

5 Center and sew soutache over the tuck stitching lines, finishing the ends neatly. Unfold the drawstring ends from inside the cover. Press the tucks toward the drawstring ends. ▽

6 Using a safety pin or small bodkin as a guide, thread a drawstring through each casing. Put the cover on the bolster and draw up the fabric. Cut two small pieces of fabric, insert one through the opening at each end; tack to the casing if desired.

center rounds

ABOUT THE SAMPLES

Each cover is a tube gathered on the front and back of the form with a drawstring; the drawstring casings are covered with fabric rosettes and covered buttons. Both covers are printed cotton; the stripes on one run around the tube; on the other, up and down it. The round forms are 13" in diameter and 2½" thick.

MATERIALS

Fabric for each pillow
Button forms to cover
Ribbon or other drawstring
Thread to match
Pillow forms

TECHNIQUES

Read About Bolsters and Rounds, pages 72–73. Refer to Part Three, Basics, for information on sewing techniques.

MEASURE, MARK, AND CUT

Note: Plan the size of the cover as explained on pages 72–73. Refer to step 1 to see how to position the stripes. The rosettes are folded in half lengthwise and gathered along the long edge; change their proportions as appropriate.

Ⓐ **PILLOW COVER** ✂cut 1 for each pillow

Ⓑ **ROSETTE** ✂cut 2 for each pillow, 4" x 17" each

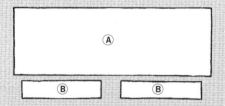

1 If you are using striped fabric, plan the position of the stripes before cutting your cover.

✂Stripes placed horizontally on the tube will form concentric circles on the front and back of the pillow. Place the center of the stripe repeat on the side of the bolster.

✂Stripes placed lengthwise on the tube will radiate from the center on the front and back. Make the cover larger than the circumference if necessary to maintain the stripe repeat across the seamline. ▽

✂Cut the rosettes so the stripes run horizontally or vertically, as complements your fabric.

TIPS FROM THE PROS

✂Because these pillows are so squat, it's easy to get confused about which are the drawstring edges and which are the seam edges. The longer edges get the drawstring, the shorter ones get sewn together to form the tube.

✂If using a lengthwise stripe (or an allover pattern or plain fabric), you don't really have to test the fit with a sample—just cut the cover a little longer than you think you need it, make the drawstring in one end, then calculate the length needed and cut off any excess fabric.

✂If you'd prefer this pillow without the rosettes, be sure the gap left inside the gathers is small enough to be concealed by the button.

Fabric rosettes and big covered buttons make a sprightly mask for the gap at the center of the drawstring closures on these round covers.

2 Place each cover (A) right side up. Draw lines on each long edge for the casing as you did to make your drawstring fit test.

3 With the wrong side out, fold each cover in half, bringing the short edges together. Sew the short edges together, leaving the seam open at each end between the marked lines; backstitch on each side of each opening to reinforce the seam for the drawstring. ▽

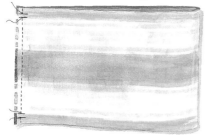

4 On each cover finish all the cut edges. Press the seam open. At each end fold the casing allowance to the wrong side and stitch through both layers on the marked line.

5 Using a safety pin or small bodkin as a guide, thread a drawstring through each casing. Put the covers on the bolster and draw up the fabric. ▽

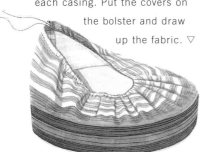

6 Fold each rosette (B) in half crosswise, wrong side out, and sew the short edges together. Press the seam open. Fold each in half lengthwise, right side out, and press the fold.

Striped fabrics make these simple covers lively. Solids would look smocked and could be wonderful with contrasting rosettes.

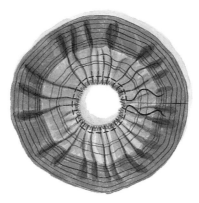

7 Finish the cut edges of each rosette together. Gather close to the finished edge (refer to Basics, page 114). Draw up as tightly as is easily possible. △

8 Center and hand sew a rosette over the drawstring casing on each side of each pillow. Cover two buttons for each pillow.

9 To attach the buttons, thread a large upholstery needle with strong thread and push it through the center of the pillow, leaving a 4"–6" tail. Pass the needle through the shank of one button, then, going through the same hole in the foam, back through the pillow; pass it through the shank of the second button. Remove the needle and tie the thread ends together with a slipknot. Tie the threads together again around the button shank and cut off the excess.

bolster sham

A shared palette turns unlike patterns into happy companions. This uneven plaid is a good choice for the flange because the stripes reinforce the geometry of the flange and the tapestry beneath.

ABOUT THE SAMPLES

The bolster cover has a button closure trimmed with a contrasting zigzag flange and welting. The sample is made of tapestry with a bias-cut silk plaid flange. The bolster shown is 23" long and 8" in diameter, with a 5½"-deep self-lined flange. Interface the flange if the fabric is lightweight.

MATERIALS

Fabrics for bolster and flange
Fusible interfacing for flange
Cable cord for welting
Thread to match
Buttons
Pillow form

TECHNIQUES

Read About Bolsters and Rounds, pages 72–73. Refer to Part Three, Basics, for information on sewing techniques.

MEASURE, MARK, AND CUT

Note: Measure the length of the bolster and add 1" for seam allowance. Measure the circumference of the bolster and add 2½" for the underlap hem and seam allowance. Cut the bolster body to these dimensions. Measure the diameter of the bolster and add 1" for seam allowance; divide this by 2 and draft a circle with this radius for the bolster end pattern (refer to Basics, page 110). To draft a pattern for the flange, refer to steps 1 and 2 of the directions.

(A) **ZIGZAG FLANGE** ✂cut 2, plus 1 from interfacing if appropriate

(B) **BOLSTER BODY** ✂cut 1

(C) **BIAS STRIPS FOR WELTING** ✂cut 1¾" wide, sufficient to rim both ends of the bolster

(D) **BOLSTER ENDS** ✂cut 2

1 Make a pattern for the flange on scrap paper. Using a square, draw a rectangle the length of the bolster by the desired depth of the flange. Divide and mark one edge in eight equal sections. At each mark, draw a line perpendicular to the edge. Use a 90-degree triangle or an L-square to draw a zigzag line as shown. ▽

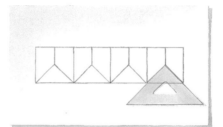

2 Check the proportions of the pattern, making the portion above the zigzag deeper or shallower as you wish. Add ½" seam allowance all around and cut out the pattern. Cut out the flange as directed.

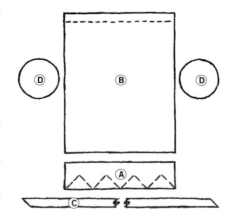

TIPS FROM THE PROS

✂To save time and minimize bias stretching, fuse interfacing to the wrong side of the fabric before cutting the flange. If you are using woven interfacing, align its bias grain with the straight grain of the flange fabric.

✂To avoid a bulky edge if you are using a heavy fabric for the flange, line it with something lighter in weight and omit the interfacing.

3 If you have not already done so, fuse the interfacing to the wrong side of one piece of the flange. Aligning their cut edges, place the two flange pieces right sides together and sew along the zigzag edge, pivoting at each corner. Trim the seam allowance at the points and clip it at the inside corners.

4 Turn the flange right side out and press. Topstitch the zigzag edge. Parallel to and 2" below the long cut edge mark four buttonholes; center each above a zigzag point. Make the buttonholes.

5 With the right sides together and cut edges aligned, sew the flange to the appropriate edge of the bolster body. Press the seam allowance toward the flange; topstitch. Make a 2"-deep hem at the opposite edge of the body. ▽

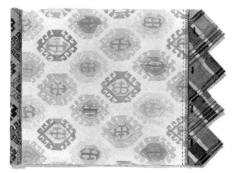

6 Make the welting. Sew welting around the right side of each bolster end; clip the flange if necessary and join the ends neatly (refer to Basics, pages 118–19). ▽

The overlap flange closure along the length transforms this otherwise ordinary bolster. You can zigzag the button band as shown, scallop it, leave it straight, or change its proportions to suit your fabrics. Consider using covered buttons or add a tassel to each zigzag point.

7 With the right sides together, pin one end of the bolster body to one of the bolster ends (refer to Basics, page 116) beginning at the edge of the zigzag flange. When you've pinned all around the circle, lap the hemmed end over the flange. Repeat to pin the other end. Check that the hem overlap is even at both ends; adjust the pins if necessary. Sew the ends to the body. ▷

8 Turn the bolster cover right side out. Sew a button opposite each buttonhole. Insert the bolster form.

tied firecracker bolster

MEASURE, MARK, AND CUT

Note: Measure the circumference of the bolster. Measure and add together the length and diameter of the bolster to find the distance between the wrapped ties; add to this twice the desired length of the firecracker end. Add twice the seam allowance to both measurements and cut the main cover this size. Cut the facings the same width as the main cover and deep enough to extend under the wrap. Cut the band as wide as desired and as long as the circumference plus twice the seam allowance.

Ⓐ CONTRASTING BAND ✂cut 1
Ⓑ MAIN COVER ✂cut 1
Ⓒ FACING ✂cut 2

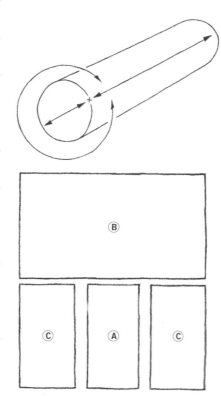

1 Press under the seam allowance on both long edges of the contrasting band (A). Mark the midpoint on each end. Place the main cover right side up. Mark the midpoint on each long edge.

TIPS FROM THE PROS

✂The band on our pillow is trimmed with cord sewn on by hand. If you'd rather use piping with a flange, sew it to the right side of the long edges of the band before pressing them under.

The tassels and cord tying this cover closed are easy to put together, but when you're shopping for fabric look first in the drapery department, where you might find suitable ready-made tiebacks. Alternatively, use ribbon, twill tape, or lace for the ties.

2 Center the contrasting band right side up over the main cover (B), matching the marked midpoints; baste together along the cut edges. Edgestitch the sides of the band to the cover. ▽

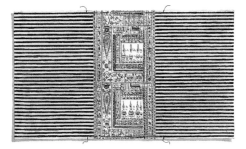

3 Lay decorative cording along the edge of the contrasting band and sew in place by hand.

4 Finish one long edge of each facing (C). With the right sides together and cut edges aligned, sew a facing to each end of the main cover. ▽

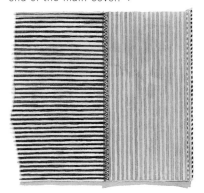

5 Press the seams open. Fold the cover in half lengthwise, wrong side out. Sew the long edges together. ▽

6 Press the seam open. With the cover still wrong side out, fold the facings to the wrong side and press the seamed edges sharply. ▽

7 Turn the cover right side out. Insert the bolster form. Wrap decorative cord around each end to form the firecracker effect, and tie in a bow or knot. Sew a tassel to each end of the cord.

Whether you use dressy or informal fabrics for this cover, you won't need much for the applied band, so pick something special— this one is a souvenir from a trip to Egypt.

TIPS FROM THE PROS

✄Here's a nice way to put the tasseled ties together: Cut the decorative cord to twice the length desired. Fold it into a flat loop, overlapping the cut ends in the middle. Position and secure a tassel at each end of the loop (slide the tassels over the cord if possible), then knot or sew the ends of the cord together. ▽

gift-wrapped bolster

ABOUT THE SAMPLE

The bolster cover is a tube of slubbed silk. The bolster shown is 25" long and 7" square. See the tip at right for a quick way to make a square bolster.

MATERIALS

Fabric

Frog closures

Thread to match

Pillow form

TECHNIQUES

Read About Bolsters and Rounds, pages 72–73. Refer to Part Three, Basics, for information on sewing techniques.

MEASURE, MARK, AND CUT

Note: Measure the length of the bolster and add to it twice the width. Measure the circumference of the bolster and add twice the seam allowance. Cut the cover to these dimensions; the length includes an allowance of half the width for a self-facing at each end.

Ⓐ **BOLSTER COVER** ✂ cut 1

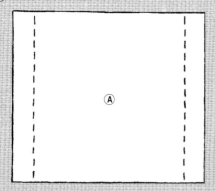

TIPS FROM THE PROS

✂ Square bolsters are not so easy to find. Here's a quick way to make one: Have several slabs of foam cut to the length and width you want the bolster to be, then stack them to achieve the desired height. Glue them together or secure them in a muslin wrapper.

1 Fold the cover in half lengthwise, wrong side out. Sew the long edges together. ▽

2 Press the seam open and finish the ends of the tube.

TIPS FROM THE PROS

✂ To avoid creating a ridge that will show through the cover, finish the ends with a serger or zigzag stitch; don't turn under the edges. If you don't have the equipment to do this, pink the edges or leave them raw.

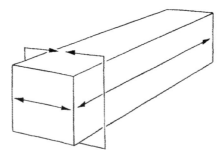

A striped fabric enhances the ends of this pillow cover, where it folds naturally into a mitered pattern. Consider changing the proportions and putting this wrapper on a conventional boxed pillow—the ends will become the top and bottom.

3 With the cover still wrong side out, fold the facing allowance at each end to the wrong side and baste the edges to secure temporarily. ▽

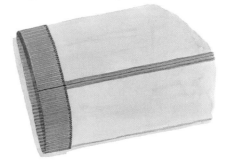

4 Turn the cover right side out and slide it over the bolster form so it extends evenly at both ends. Position the seam along one edge of the form.

5 At each end, fold two opposite edges onto the form; they should butt in the middle and form a triangular point at the top and bottom of the form. △

6 Fold the points onto the end of the form and tack together. Sew a decorative frog closure over the points. ▽

This truly is a beginner's project—it's got only one seam, the ends are folded and tacked closed, and then decorated with purchased frogs.

drawstring **treasure** ball

ABOUT THE SAMPLE

The pillow cover is a tube gathered onto a circle at one end; the other end has a self-faced flange and is gathered with a cord passed through ribbon loops. The circumference of the pillow is about 36"; the flange is 4½" deep. Begin with a drawstring cord equal to the pillow circumference plus 12"; cut off any excess after tying as desired.

MATERIALS

Fabric
Decorative cord or other drawstring
Ribbon for drawstring carrier loops
Thread to match
Pillow form or muslin and stuffing

TECHNIQUES

Read About Bolsters and Rounds, pages 72–73. Refer to Part Three, Basics, for information on sewing techniques.

MEASURE, MARK, AND CUT

Note: Refer to step 1 to draft the pattern. If you wish to make rather than purchase the pillow form, the directions are given under steps 1–4; make it before cutting the cover.

(A) **BOTTOM** ✂cut 2 each for the form and cover

(B) **PILLOW FORM BODY** ✂cut 1

(C) **PILLOW COVER BODY** ✂cut 1

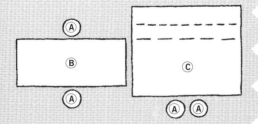

1 Draft the patterns. You can draw them directly onto the fabric or onto a piece of paper first. If you wish to make the pillow form, first decide the circumference of the finished ball. Refer to the drawings, below left.
✂For the bottom (A), draft a circle with a circumference equal to half the circumference of the pillow form (refer to Basics, page 110). Add seam allowance.
✂For the form body (B), draw a rectangle. Make the length equal to the desired circumference, and the width equal to half the circumference minus the radius of the bottom circle. Add seam allowance all around.
✂For the pillow cover body (C), measure the circumference of your form. Draw a rectangle this long and half this wide. Decide how deep to make the flange and draw a line this distance from and parallel to the long edge; label it as the foldline. Add 2" to the flange depth and draw a third line this distance from the foldline. Add ½" seam allowance to the three other edges.

2 With the right sides together and cut edges aligned, sew the short edges of the pillow cover body together. Press the seam open and sew gathering stitches at one end of the tube. Draw up the gathering threads.
✂For the form, leave an opening in the middle of the seam and sew gathers at both ends of the tube.

Bottom up or down—this pillow is fun from any angle. In fact, if you like the end with the sewn-on round best, skip the outer cover and just make the pillow form in your chosen fabric. In either case, the round could contrast with the main fabric.

3 Pin and sew the gathered end to one of the bottom circles.
✂For the form, sew a circle at each end of the tube. ▽

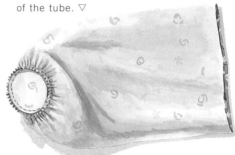

4 Press the seam allowance onto the bottom circle.
✂For the form, turn the assembled pieces right side out, fill with loose stuffing, and slipstitch the opening closed.

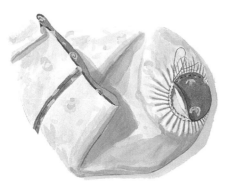

5 For the bottom lining, press the seam allowance of the remaining circle to the wrong side. Pin and hand sew the lining to the bottom of the tube. △

TIPS FROM THE PROS

✄ To more easily turn under the edge of a circle, first sew gathering stitches in the seam allowance, then pull the gathers up slightly and press the allowance under.

✄ To give the bottom circle a smooth edge, cut a piece of quilter's template plastic the same size and place it against the wrong side of the bottom before sewing on the lining.

6 Finish the edge of the open end of the tube. Press the self-facing to the wrong side along the foldline. Insert the pillow form and check that the facing extends below the top of the form; adjust if necessary. Remove the form. Baste the facing in place about 2" above the finished edge. ▽

This witty pillow is made like a drawstring bag. If you wish, skip the inner form and encourage your kids to stuff the cover with their pajamas.

7 From the ribbon cut six pieces for the drawstring carrier loops; make them long enough to turn under at each end and ride easily over the cord. Press under both ends of each carrier.

8 Turn the cover right side out. Center the loops over the basting, placing them perpendicular to the stitching and spacing them evenly around the tube. Topstitch across each end of each loop. ▷

9 Insert the pillow form. Pass the cord under the loops, pull it up, and tie a knot or bow.

flat-sided bolsters

ABOUT THE SAMPLES

Welting is sewn between the rectangular panels that cover the sides of these bolsters. The 36"-long wedge bolster is 10½" high, 8½" wide at the bottom, and 6½" wide at the top. The 20"-long triangular bolster is 7" wide on each side. The fabrics are cotton plaid and lightweight denim.

MATERIALS

Fabric(s)
Cable cord for welting
Thread to match
Pillow form(s)

TECHNIQUES

Read About Bolsters and Rounds, pages 72–73. Refer to Part Three, Basics, for information on foam pillow forms and sewing techniques.

MEASURE, MARK, AND CUT

Note: Have foam forms cut to the desired size. To determine the size to cut the side panels, measure the sides of the forms and add seam allowance to each edge. To make a pattern for each end shape, trace the end of each form on scrap paper and add seam allowance to each edge.

(A) **BIAS STRIPS FOR WELTING** ✂cut 1³/4" **wide, sufficient to rim all the seams**

(B) **WEDGE BACK PANEL** ✂cut 1

(C) **WEDGE FRONT PANEL** ✂cut 1

(D) **WEDGE TOP PANEL** ✂cut 1

(E) **WEDGE BOTTOM PANEL** ✂cut 1

(F) **WEDGE ENDS** ✂cut 2, reversing 1

(G) **TRIANGLE SIDE PANELS** ✂cut 3

(H) **TRIANGLE ENDS** ✂cut 2

FOR EITHER PILLOW

1 From the bias strips (A), make the welting (refer to Basics, page 118).

2 With the right sides together and cut edges aligned, sew welting to one long edge of each bolster panel (B, C, D, and E) or (G). At each end, cut the cord from inside the welting and swing the welting across the seamline (refer to Basics, page 118). ▽

3 With the right sides together and cut edges aligned, sew together the panels for the bolster, forming a tube. If you are making the wedge, be sure you join the panels in the proper sequence. Begin and end the seams ½" from each end of each panel; reinforce with backstitching. Leave a long opening on one seam for inserting the pillow form later.

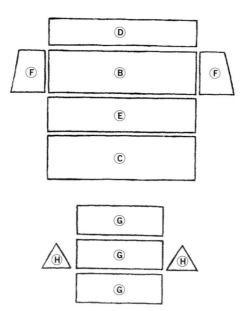

Plain denim was chosen for the ends of these bolsters not only because it looks great but because matching the plaid from the slanted sides would be impossible.

4 With the right sides together and cut edges aligned, sew welting around the perimeter of each end piece (F) or (H); clip the welting flange at each corner and overlap the ends in the middle of one edge, finishing them neatly (refer to Basics, page 119). ▽

5 With the right sides together and cut edges aligned, sew an end piece to each end of the bolster tube as follows: Leaving all the seam allowances free, sew each edge of the end to the corresponding edge of the tube separately; stop and start at the adjacent seamline at each corner. ▷

6 Insert the pillow form and slipstitch the opening closed.

TIPS FROM THE PROS

✂ You'll find it easier to sew the opening closed if you use a large curved needle.

A sturdy wedge bolster offers good back support—use it on a daybed or window seat. The smaller triangular bolster is fun to toss around; make it any size you like.

about cushions for furniture

Sewing cushions for furniture is really no different from sewing any other sort of pillow; the pieces are just likely to be larger. With the exception of the bolsters, virtually any pillow in this book could be made for the seat of a chair or bench—indeed, some of the projects in the previous chapters are shown used in this manner. While square-edge styles are the most common choice for furniture, knife-edge pillows make good kitchen chair pads and, in the right scale and fabrication, can be effective, if somewhat eccentric, in other settings.

To transform a throw pillow into a cushion, all you really have to do is adjust the proportions to suit the furniture. Refer to About Knife-Edge Pillows, pages 24–25, and About Square-Edge Pillows, pages 56–57, for basic construction directions. If you wish to make a round cushion, for instance to top a stool, refer to About Bolsters and Rounds, pages 72–73, and follow the directions for making a closed-end bolster. On the following pages you'll find directions for six cushion projects.

CHOOSING FABRIC

Cover cushions in fabric that will hold up to the stress of being sat upon. Decorator fabrics are a good choice. Keeping this in mind, choose any fabric that pleases you and trim it as you wish. If your cushions are for outdoor furniture, consider a fabric that has a protective coating, or spray one on when the cushions are finished. Be aware that most fabrics will fade with constant exposure to sunlight.

SIZING THE FORM

The key to successful cushion making is a form that fits the furniture properly. If you are making a cushion for a bench that has neither arms nor a back, it is probably sufficient to just measure the seat and have a piece of foam cut to the same dimensions. In most other instances, you'll be off to a better start if you make a muslin or paper template and have the foam cut to match.

✂ If you wish to use a form filled with loose stuffing, measure or make a template as described above and make the form using the measurements or the template as a cutting guide.

✂ If you are making a knife-edge cushion that you plan to stuff plumply, make it a bit larger than the surface it will cover. Once stuffed, the cushion will become rounded and the edges will lift, making it appear skimpy on the seat.

Whatever sort of cushion you are making, always check the fit of the form on the furniture before cutting and making the cover. Adjust the form if necessary. For more information, read About Pillow Forms, page 112.

Sizing Back Cushions

If you are making a back as well as a seat cushion, plan the size of both at once. Usually the seat cushion should extend under the back cushion; if the back cushion extends behind the seat cushion, the seat cushion is likely to slide forward when you sit on it. When you measure for the back cushion, be sure to subtract the thickness of the seat cushion from the height. Place a piece of masking tape across the back of the chair at this level as a reminder.

Selecting a Thickness for the Form

How thick should a cushion be? Does it matter? In some situations the thickness of the cushion is purely a matter of preference—and comfort. In others, the proportions of the furniture may dictate this dimension. Here are some pointers:

✂ Always consider the proportions of the furniture when determining the seat cushion thickness. A seat cushion should not obscure or spoil the design or proportions of the chair back.

✂ Chair pads can be very thin. In fact, they can be made like placemats, stuffed only with a sheet of batting or very thin foam. When made this way they're usually washable.

✂ Foam cushions are usually 2"–4" thick. Anything more is likely to raise the seat level too high for comfort.

✂ If the chair back or arms slant or curve away from the seat, make the seat cushion thinner rather than thicker; otherwise there will be gaps around it. Or opt for a slightly oversize soft cushion that can be squished to fit as needed.

✂ If you are making a boxed cushion, consider the fabric before selecting a cushion thickness. You might want the boxing—and thus the thickness—to accommodate a stripe or other motif.

TIPS FROM THE PROS

✂ Check the fit of a foam form before you wrap it with batting. The batting will be condensed by the cover, so it won't affect the fit.

SIZING THE COVER

A cushion cover should fit snuggly over its form. If it is loose it will wrinkle, crease, and be sloppy after it's been sat upon. If you'd like a cushion to look more casual than tailored, make a knife-edge or dart-shaped cover over a form filled with loose stuffing or have a down-filled form made.

Sizing Covers for Foam Forms

Because it should fit tightly, there are a few tricks to sizing a cushion cover for a foam form. Some people measure the form and draft patterns that are about $1/2$" smaller in each direction. Another approach is to take the measurements before the foam is wrapped in batting; the batting will add some extra volume to tighten the fit of the cover. Whichever method you choose, be sure to do your math to see that the boxing fits each side of the cushion properly.

CLOSING CUSHION COVERS

The least obvious way to close a cushion cover is by slipstitching the section of the seam left open so the form could be inserted. However, the slipstitches have to be removed and replaced every time the cover is cleaned. The best method for making a cushion cover easily removable varies with the type of cover. Some closures must be planned before the cover is cut, so read the following first. Zipper installation is explained on pages 120–21.

Closing a Knife-Edge Cover

Close a knife-edge cushion cover with an overlap closure on the bottom; refer to page 117. Alternatively, install a slot zipper on the cushion bottom.

To prepare for this, cut the bottom in two sections, adding seam allowance to all edges. Be aware, however, that if the cushion is plump, both closures will be visible from the side unless there is a flange, ruffle, or deep fringe hanging down from the perimeter seam.

Closing a Dart-Shaped Cover

Close a dart–shaped cushion cover with a zipper inserted in a portion of the perimeter seam. Insert the zipper on one side before sewing the cushion top and bottom together along the three remaining sides.

TIPS FROM THE PROS

✄ It's difficult to sew the perimeter seam right up to the zipper ends after the zipper is installed. Instead, when basting the seam closed prior to installing the zipper, permanently sew a small section beyond each end of the basted portion.

✄ To create an opening for turning the finished cushion right side out, be sure to open the zipper before sewing the remaining sides together.

Closing a Boxed Cover

Close a boxed cushion cover with a slot zipper centered between the cushion top and bottom on a portion of the boxing. To do this you must plan for the zipper as explained below before you cut the boxing. Alternatively, make an overlap closure on the cushion bottom; refer to page 117.

To accommodate the zipper, measure and cut the boxing as follows:

✄ On the sides of the cushion make a mark 2" forward from the back corners.

✄ For the front boxing, measure from mark to mark around the front of the cushion and add 9" for seam allowance and two 2"-deep pleats. Measure the thickness of the cushion and add 1". Cut a band with these dimensions.

✄ For the back boxing, measure from mark to mark across the back of the cushion and add 1" for seam allowance. Measure the thickness of the cushion and add 2". Cut a band with these dimensions; cut this band in half lengthwise. ▽

Insert a slot zipper on the back boxing; do not extend the zipper into the end seam allowances. Sew the ends of the back boxing to the ends of the front boxing, forming a ring. At each seam fold a 2"-deep pleat in the front boxing, folding it over the back boxing. Baste the pleats along the edges. ▽

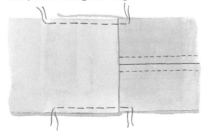

Sew the boxing to the cushion top in the usual manner; open the zipper and sew the boxing to the cushion back. Turn the cover right side out through the zipper.

ABOUT THE SAMPLE

The back and seat cushion covers are printed cotton; a contrasting check fabric covers the welting and the long rectangular arm pad. Each cushion is shaped with small tucks along the perimeter. Each cushion form has a 2"-thick foam core supplemented with loose stuffing.

MATERIALS

Fabrics
Cable cord for welting
Thread to match
Foam, loose polyester stuffing, and muslin for forms
Batting for arm pad

TECHNIQUES

Read About Cushions for Furniture, pages 88–89. Refer to Part Three, Basics, for information on making pillow forms and other sewing techniques.

MEASURE, MARK, AND CUT

Note: Refer to the directions to make the patterns and pillow forms. Measure for the arm pad as shown in the diagram at right.

Ⓐ **SEAT CUSHION TOP & BOTTOM** ✂cut 2 from muslin, 2 from decorative fabric

Ⓑ **BACK CUSHION FRONT & BACK** ✂cut 2 from muslin, 2 from decorative fabric

Ⓒ **BIAS STRIPS FOR WELTING** ✂cut 1³/₄" wide, enough to go around perimeter of both cushions

Ⓓ **ARM PAD COVER** ✂cut 2 from decorative fabric, 1 from batting

CUSHION FORMS

1 To determine the cushion shapes, lay pieces of muslin over the seat and back of the chair. Trace the outline of each shape; you'll have to trim and slash the muslin over each arm in order to get it to lie smoothly. ▽

2 Remove the muslin from the chair. Fold each piece in half lengthwise. True up the shapes (refer to Basics, page 111) and round all the corners. Cut out each shape on the final outline.

3 Determine the thickness of the seat cushion and trim this amount from the bottom of the back muslin. Place each muslin shape on 2"-thick foam, draw around it, and cut out the foam.

4 To make the pattern for the cushion forms, center the foam for each cushion on a piece of muslin. Draw around it. Remove the foam. Divide the desired cushion thickness by 2. Draw another line parallel to and this distance outside the first for the seamline. Draw a third line ¹/₂" outside the second for the cutting line. Cut out the form patterns. ▽

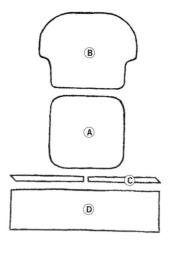

✄It's difficult to judge the amount of fabric needed to create a shaped cushion like the one on the back of this chair—especially if your chair back curves from side to side. So that you can adjust the fit easily, cut the form pattern without seam allowance, then, in the next step, trace around it to mark the seamline and add a generous seam allowance when cutting the form.

5 From each form pattern cut two identical muslin pieces and transfer the seamline to each. On each, sew gathering stitches along the seamline around each corner. Place one of the muslin pieces wrong side up and center the corresponding piece of foam on it. Adjust the gathering stitches until the seamline on the muslin is just a little larger than the perimeter of the foam. Transfer the foam to the matching piece of muslin and repeat. Repeat with the remaining foam and muslin. ▽

6 Remove the foam from the muslin. Aligning the cut edges, pin and machine baste each muslin pair together on the seamline; leave an opening on the back or bottom edge. Leave the covers wrong side out and insert the foam. Fill each cover by inserting loose stuffing on both sides of the foam; pin the opening closed.

Plump, contoured cushions and draped arm pads mask the rough surface of a wicker chair. Use them indoors or out.

7 Check the fit of the seat cushion form on the chair and adjust if necessary. With the seat cushion form on the chair, check the fit of the back cushion form and adjust if necessary.
✄If the cushion forms are too big, open the seam in the appropriate area, remove some of the stuffing, and pin a new seamline. Try to refine the fit by adjusting the amount of loose stuffing before trimming the foam.

✄If the cushion forms are too small, open the seam in the appropriate area, add more stuffing, and pin a new seamline.
✄Remove the stuffing and foam. Transfer any changes to your muslin patterns so you'll be able to cut the decorative covers (if you've made the covers larger, tape or baste additional muslin to the pattern). Sew the new seams where marked.

comfy armchair cushions

To tie this set together, use one fabric for the cushion covers, another for the welting and arm pads. Here a vintage-style fruit print is paired with a classic check.

TIPS FROM THE PROS

✄You may not be able to stuff the lower portion of the back as plumply as the upper portion—too much stuffing will cause the fabric to strain along the inside curve of the T. The foam slab will support the extra weight at the top and keep the cushion from sagging.

✄Be safe, not lazy. If you've made significant adjustments to the forms, relax the gathers and flatten the covers so you can accurately transfer the new seamlines to the patterns; make new patterns if necessary.

8 Clip the inside curves and turn the muslin covers right side out. Stuff as before. Slipstitch the openings closed.

CUSHION COVERS

1 Using the patterns made for the forms, cut out the decorative covers (A and B); be sure to include $1/2$" seam allowance all around each piece. Place one piece of a decorative cover, centered, over a corresponding cushion form; pin in a few places. To contour the decorative cover, pin several tucks along the seamline at each corner. Remove the cover and duplicate the tucks on the matching cover piece. Repeat with the remaining decorative cover and cushion form. Baste the tucks on each seamline. ▽

2 Make the welting (C). With the right sides together and cut edges aligned, sew welting around the perimeter of one piece of the seat cushion cover and one piece of the back cushion cover; join and finish the welting ends neatly (refer to Basics, pages 118–19). ▽

3 With the right sides together and cut edges aligned, pin and sew the decorative cover pieces together in pairs along the welting seamline; use a zipper foot and leave an opening on the back and bottom edges.

4 Press the seams open. Turn the covers right side out. Insert each cushion form in the corresponding decorative cover, and slipstitch the openings closed.

ARM PAD

1 With the right sides together and cut edges aligned, place the pieces of the arm pad (D) on your worktable. Top with the batting. Pin and baste together around the perimeter. ▽

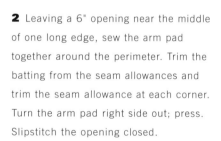

2 Leaving a 6" opening near the middle of one long edge, sew the arm pad together around the perimeter. Trim the batting from the seam allowances and trim the seam allowance at each corner. Turn the arm pad right side out; press. Slipstitch the opening closed.

3 If desired, mark the width of the chair seat on the center of each long edge of the pad, draw lines across the pad to connect the marks, and sew on the lines through all layers. ▽

bench pillow

1 Place the muslin foundation (A) right side up; mark the midpoint on each end. Mark the midpoint on each end of the tapestry panel (B). Center the panel right side up on the muslin, matching the marked midpoints. Baste the panel to the muslin. ▽

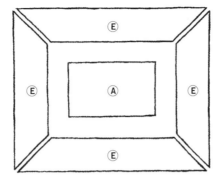

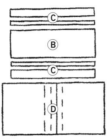

This knife-edge cushion has a deep flange that serves as a skirt. The flange combines the geometry of a miter with the bias of a soft fabric to create a graceful corner.

ABOUT THE SAMPLE

The pillow top has a muslin foundation that is covered with one band of tapestry and two bands each of two fancy ribbons. The flange is soft velvet. The back is plain cotton. The sample is 12" x 20", with an 8"-deep flange. Select tapestry and ribbons wide enough to completely cover the top.

MATERIALS

Muslin for foundation
Tapestry panel and ribbons
Fabric for flange and back
Narrow decorative trim
Thread to match
Desired fastener for back closure
Muslin and stuffing for pillow form

TECHNIQUES

Read About Cushions for Furniture, pages 88–89. Refer to Part Three, Basics, for information on overlap closures and other sewing techniques.

MEASURE, MARK, AND CUT

Note: Measure your bench and make a knife-edge pillow form to fit it (refer to page 112). Cut the muslin top to fit the pillow form, adding seam allowance. Cut the back wide enough to allow for an overlap closure. To determine the width to cut the flange panels, allow 8" for gathers on the top edge of each flange panel and plan for bias side seams; cut the panels as rectangles and trim after sewing together.

Ⓐ **PILLOW TOP FOUNDATION** ✂cut 1
Ⓑ **TAPESTRY PANEL** ✂cut 1
Ⓒ **RIBBON BANDS** ✂cut 4, or as appropriate, making each the length of the pillow top
Ⓓ **PILLOW BACK** ✂cut 1
Ⓔ **FLANGE** ✂cut 4, as deep as desired

shirred-flange bench pillow

2 Pin a band of ribbon (C) on each side of the tapestry panel; overlap the tapestry with the ribbon. Edgestitch along the overlapped edges. Baste the outer edge of the ribbons to the muslin. ▷

3 Repeat as necessary to cover the muslin with ribbon.

TIPS FROM THE PROS

✂ The direction in which you overlap the ribbon is not important—lap yours as best suits their edges. To be sure you like the arrangement, baste them all in place before edgestitching any.

4 Make the overlap closure on the pillow back (D), trimming the back to the same size as the top, applying the fastening, and pinning the overlap closed at the hem ends (refer to Basics, page 117).

5 Finish the raw bottom edge of each flange panel (E) to prepare it for hemming later. Using a 45-degree right-angle triangle and marking on the wrong side of the fabric, draw a bias seamline from bottom to top at each end of each panel. At the bottom edge, reverse the triangle to mark a line perpendicular to this through the hem. ▽

If this look doesn't suit your decor, try a different fabrication. For instance, pair a solid top with a floral stripe that miters interestingly or marry vintage linens with heavy lace. Note that in the right proportions, with a shallower flange, this design would be a pretty throw pillow.

6 Place an end and side panel right sides together with their bottom edges toward you on your worktable. At the right end, pin the panels together, aligning the marked seamlines and placing the pins so you can remove them easily when sewing from top to bottom. ▽

7 Repeat to pin all the side seams, pinning a side panel between each end panel and being sure always to pin so you can sew from top to bottom.

8 Sew the side seams, pivoting onto the marked seamline at the hem edge. Cut off the excess fabric, finish the seam allowance edges, and trim the points as shown. ▽

TIPS FROM THE PROS

✂ To ensure that the flange will turn around each corner when you pin it to the pillow top, begin stitching the side seams just above the top seamline, not at the cut edge.

✂ If your flange is velvet, baste the seams first. Then sew using a velvet foot on your machine—this very narrow foot puts the least possible pressure on the fabric and minimizes scars from the machine feed.

✂ The weight of the fabric can cause bias seams to stretch. To prevent these seams from binding and appearing puckered, pull the fabric taut as you sew.

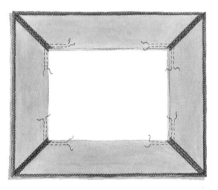

9 Hem the bottom of the flange by hand or machine as appropriate. On the top edge, beginning and ending about 5" from the seam, sew gathers around each corner (refer to Basics, page 114). △

10 With the right sides together and cut edges aligned, pin the flange to the pillow top, aligning a side seam with each corner of the top. Baste the flange to the top by hand or machine. ▽

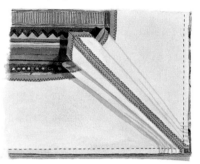

11 Place the pillow form on the bench. Lay the pillow top right side up over it. Check that the gathers hang nicely at the corners; adjust if necessary.

12 Remove the pillow top from the bench. Place it right side up on your worktable. Fold the flange onto the center again, as it was in step 10. Aligning their cut edges, place the overlapped pillow back (with the hem ends basted closed) wrong side up over the top and flange. Pin and sew the back to the top.

13 Trim the corner seam allowance. Also trim any excess bulk from the seam allowance of the overlapped hems. Turn the pillow cover right side out.

14 By hand sew decorative trim around the perimeter of the pillow top. Insert the pillow form.

easy hinged cushions

ABOUT THE SAMPLE

Each of the softly boxed cushions is made from two rectangles of print fabric. A fabric hinge is inserted in the back seam of the seat cushion and the bottom seam of the back cushion. The cushions are about 4" thick; the back cushion is tufted with buttons.

MATERIALS

Fabric

Buttons with shank backs; a pair for each position

Thread to match

Foam or other materials for cushion forms

TECHNIQUES

Read About Cushions for Furniture, pages 88–89. Refer to Part Three, Basics, for information on making pillow forms and other sewing techniques.

MEASURE, MARK, AND CUT

Note: For the cushion forms, measure the length and width of the chair seat; measure the length and width of the chair back above the level of the seat cushion. Have a foam cushion cut to each of these dimensions, or make mock-boxed pillow forms (refer to page 112). For the cushion covers, measure lengthwise and widthwise around each form; divide each dimension in half and add twice the seam allowance. Cut the cover pieces to the last dimensions. The finished hinge should be about 3" narrower than the back by the thickness of one cushion.

Ⓐ **BACK CUSHION FRONT & BACK** ✂cut 2

Ⓑ **SEAT CUSHION TOP & BOTTOM** ✂cut 2

Ⓒ **HINGE** ✂cut 2

TIPS FROM THE PROS

✂If you wish to use foam forms, begin with foam that is about half the desired thickness; wrap the forms in several layers of batting to build them up and soften their edges.

1 To find the length to make the corner darts, measure the thickness of your pillow forms; divide this dimension in half. For example, if your pillow form is 4" thick, the corner dart will be 2" long.

2 Place each of the pillow cover pieces (A and B) wrong side up. At each corner, mark the seam allowance along the edges. From each marked corner, measure and mark the length of the dart on each seamline. ▽

Exuberant prints are wonderful choices for outdoor cushions, but if that's not what you have in mind, these would look sharp and classic in a solid color.

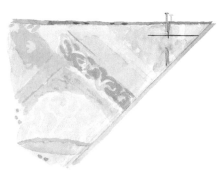

3 At each corner fold the fabric diagonally, wrong side out, aligning the adjacent cut edges (fold along the dash line in the drawing at left). Perpendicular to the cut edge, place a pin through the mark made in the last step. △

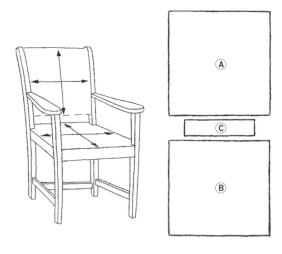

Paired cushions won't lose their mates if they're joined with a fabric hinge. This design is ideal for pieces that will sometimes be stored and for use on reclining furniture; the hinge allows the cushions to flex as needed.

4 Keeping the fabric wrong side out, slide your fingers between the layers to open one boxed corner. Flatten and center the dart over the pinned corner; pin as shown, keeping the pin heads below the cut side edges. Repeat at each corner. △

5 Remove the pins inserted in step 3. From the right side, trim the points of fabric extending above the cut side edges. Baste across the end of each dart to secure it.

6 With right sides together and cut edges aligned, sew the hinge pieces (C) together at both ends. ▽

7 Turn the hinge right side out. With the right sides together, center one long hinge edge on the bottom edge of one piece of the back cushion. Center the other long hinge edge on the back edge of one piece of the seat cushion. Pin and sew together. ▷

8 With the right sides together, sew the back cushion pieces together, leaving an opening along the hinge. Sew the seat cushion pieces together in the same way. Press the seams open and turn the covers right side out. Insert the forms and slipstitch the openings closed.

9 Put the cushions on the chair and mark the button placements. Thread a long sturdy needle with heavy thread. At each mark, insert the needle all the way through the cushion, pull it through, leaving a long tail of thread on both sides, and remove the needle. Repeat about 1/4" away. On one side of the cushion, tie a square knot; leave the thread tails hanging. Repeat on the other side, pulling the thread tight to indent the cushion.

10 At each indent, pass one thread end through a button shank and tie securely to the other thread end. Cut off the excess threads.

chair pad

ABOUT THE SAMPLE

The boxing of this shaped pad is pieced on each side of the back post cutouts; a tie is inserted into each seam. If your chair seat does not require back post cutouts, piece the boxing at both back corners and insert a pair of ties in each seam. The pad is 2½" thick; it is covered in mattress ticking and rimmed with self-welting.

MATERIALS

Fabric
Cable cord for welting
Thread to match
Foam for cushion form

TECHNIQUES

Read About Cushions for Furniture, pages 88–89. Refer to Part Three, Basics, for information on making pillow forms and other sewing techniques.

MEASURE, MARK, AND CUT

Note: Make a template of your chair seat and from it make a foam form. To make the pattern for the pad top and bottom, trace the outline of the form and add seam allowance all around. For the boxing, cut a strip the length of each edge, adding seam allowance all around.

Ⓐ **BIAS STRIPS FOR WELTING** ✂cut 1¾" wide, sufficient to rim perimeter of top and bottom

Ⓑ **PAD TOP & BOTTOM** ✂cut 2

Ⓒ **TIES** ✂cut 4, each 2" x 15"; cut on the bias, if desired

Ⓓ **BACK POST BOXING STRIPS** ✂cut 2

Ⓔ **BACK BOXING STRIP** ✂cut 1

Ⓕ **SIDE/FRONT/SIDE BOXING STRIP** ✂cut 1

1 Make the welting (A). With the right sides together and cut edges aligned, sew welting around the perimeter of the pad top and pillow bottom (B); overlap the ends on the back edge and finish them neatly. (Refer to Basics, pages 118–19.) ▽

2 Make four ties; leave one end of each open (refer to Basics, page 120). With the right sides together and cut edges aligned, center and sew a tie to each end of each back post boxing strip (D). ▷

Narrow ties anchor this pad to the chair. For a different look, make the ties the same width as the boxing—or even wider—they'll create big festive bows.

TIPS FROM THE PROS

✂If your pad does not require back post boxing strips, sew two ties to each end of the back boxing strip at this time.

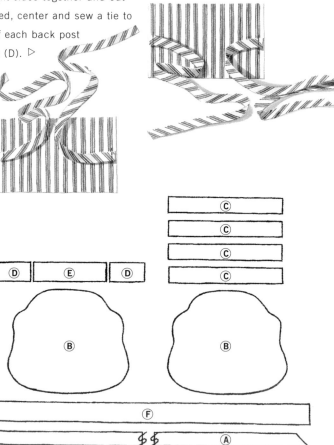

3 With the right sides together and cut edges aligned, sew a back post boxing strip to each end of the back boxing strip (E). Sew the ends of the side/front/side boxing strip (F) to the other ends of the back post boxing strips, forming a ring. ▽

TIPS FROM THE PROS
✂Plan ahead so you'll be able to pivot easily when you sew the boxing to the pad top and bottom: Stitch the boxing strip seams between the top and bottom seam allowances only, backstitching at each end.

4 With the right sides together and cut edges aligned, pin the boxing to the pad top. Test the fit on the pad; adjust the length and/or depth of the boxing if necessary. Sew the boxing to the top. Clip the curves and corners as necessary (refer to Basics, page 116). ▽

You can make this classic chair pad in virtually any fabric; we chose ticking for the way its stripes create subtle vibrations when they intersect vertically, horizontally, and diagonally.

TIPS FROM THE PROS
✂Because you'll be sewing both inside and outside curves or corners, you'll find it easier to sew the boxing to the pad top if you hand baste the pieces together first.

5 In the same manner, sew the pad bottom to the other edge of the boxing; leave an opening along the back edge. Trim the excess seam allowance at the corners. Press the seams toward the pad top and bottom. Turn the cover right side out, insert the pillow form, and slipstitch the opening closed.

ABOUT THE SAMPLES

The tops of these 3"-thick boxed cushions are padded and simply quilted from corner to corner. They are pieced from three cotton prints.

MATERIALS

Fabrics

Cable cord for welting

Batting and muslin for quilted tops

Thread to match

Foam for cushion forms

TECHNIQUES

Read About Cushions for Furniture, pages 88–89. Refer to Part Three, Basics, for information on making pillow forms and other sewing techniques.

MEASURE, MARK, AND CUT

Note: Have a foam form cut for each cushion; be sure to measure the chair back above the seat cushion height. Refer to the directions to make the patterns for the pieced tops. Cut a piece each of batting and muslin the same size as each (sewn together) front or top. Cut as many boxing bands as needed.

Ⓐ Ⓑ **BACK CUSHION FRONT** ✄cut 2 of each triangle

Ⓒ **BIAS STRIPS FOR WELTING** ✄cut 1³/₄" wide, enough to rim top and bottom of each cushion

Ⓓ **BACK CUSHION BACK** ✄cut 1

Ⓔ **BACK CUSHION BOXING**

Ⓕ **SEAT CUSHION TOP & BOTTOM** ✄cut 2

Ⓖ **SEAT CUSHION BOXING**

Ⓗ **BENCH CUSHION TOP BANDS** ✄cut 2 of each length

Ⓘ **BENCH CUSHION TOP CENTER** ✄cut 1

Ⓙ **BENCH CUSHION BOXING**

Ⓚ **BENCH CUSHION BOTTOM** ✄cut 1

TIPS FROM THE PROS

✄If you wish to make the covers easily removable, make an overlap closure on the back of each or insert a zipper in each boxing band.

✄If you are making the whole cushion set, make all the welting at once, piece and quilt the top or front of each cushion, then complete all three assembly-line style.

CHAIR BACK CUSHION

1 To make the pattern for the cushion front, draw the outline of the form on paper; identify the top edge. Draw diagonal lines from corner to corner. If your form is not square, mark the top triangle "top/bottom" and an adjacent triangle "sides." Cut out the marked triangles and use as patterns; add seam allowance all around each when cutting. (If your form is square, the triangles will be the same; use one.) ▷

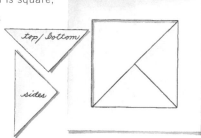

TIPS FROM THE PROS

✄Mark the adjacent edges of the triangles so you'll know which edges to sew together. Cut the fabric triangles with the hypotenuse (unmarked edge) on the straight grain.

2 With the right sides together and cut edges aligned, sew each "top" triangle (A) to a "side" triangle (B) along one edge. ▽

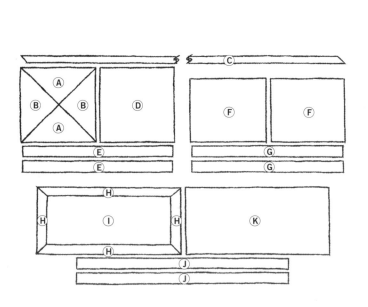

3 Press the seams open. With the right sides together and previous seams aligned, sew the paired triangles together; sew along the edge perpendicular to the previous seam. ▽

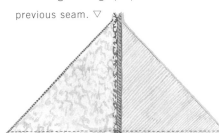

5 To quilt the front, sew through all layers, stitching from corner to corner in the ditch of the seams. ▽

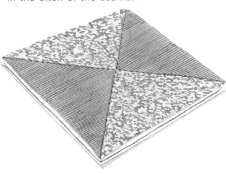

4 Press the seam open. Layer the batting over the muslin and top with the pieced front, right side up. Pin and baste together around the perimeter. △

Use variations on a theme—here fabrics and a quilted X—to tie together a set of different-size cushions.

quilted outdoor set

6 Make the welting from the bias strips (C). With right sides together and cut edges aligned, sew welting around the perimeter of the cushion front and back (D); join and finish the welting ends neatly (refer to Basics, pages 118–19).

7 With the right sides together and cut edges aligned, pin and sew the boxing (E) to the cushion front; clip and pivot the boxing at each corner (refer to Basics, page 116). Leaving an opening on one side, pin and sew the boxing to the cushion back. Trim the corners, turn the cover right side out, insert the pillow form, and slipstitch the opening closed.

CHAIR SEAT CUSHION

1 Layer the batting over the muslin, and top with the cushion top (F), right side up. Pin and baste together around the perimeter (refer to the illustration accompanying step 4 of the chair back cushion).

2 Using chalk, draw diagonal lines from corner to corner. To quilt the top, sew through all layers, stitching on the marked lines. ▽

3 Complete the seat cushion by following steps 6 and 7 of the chair back cushion; use piece G for the boxing and piece F for the cushion bottom.

BENCH CUSHION

1 To calculate the size to cut the bench cushion top pieces, first determine the depth of the perimeter band (H).
✂ To find the finished size of the center panel (I), double the band depth and subtract this dimension from the length and width of the cushion form. Cut the center to this size, adding seam allowance all around.
✂ Cut each band the desired depth and a little longer than the form edge it will trim, adding seam allowance all around. Cut the bands as rectangles; you'll trim the excess after mitering them.

2 With the right sides together and cut edges aligned, center, pin, and sew a long band to each long edge of the center panel. Begin stitching 1/2" from the end of the panel and stop 1/2" from the other end; backstitch both ends to reinforce them. Press the bands away from the center. ▽

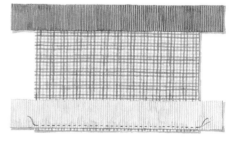

There's no point to making patchwork for the top of this seat cushion, which is partially obscured by the back cushion; just quilt a piece of fabric in a matching X.

3 In the same manner, sew a short band to each end of the center panel; stitch only between the long bands. ▽

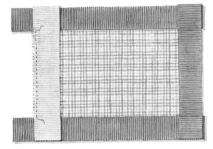

4 Turn the piece wrong side up and lap the bands as shown. Using a 45-degree right-angle triangle, mark a diagonal line from the corner of the panel seamline to the edge of the upper band. ▽

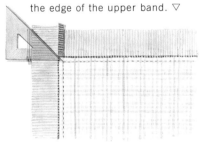

5 Reverse the lap and mark the other band in the same way. Repeat to mark the bands at each corner.

6 At one corner, fold the panel diagonally, wrong side out; fold the seam allowance toward the panel and align the seams and the marked lines. Pin and sew the bands together on the marked lines. ▽

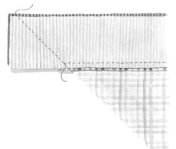

7 Repeat at each remaining corner. Trim the seam allowance; press the mitered seams open, then press the panel seams toward the bands.

8 Layer the batting over the muslin, and top with the cushion top, right side up. Pin and baste together around the perimeter (refer to the illustration accompanying step 4 of the chair back cushion).

9 Using chalk, draw diagonal lines from corner to corner of the center panel. To quilt the top, sew through all layers, stitching in the ditch of each miter seam and along the marked lines. ▷

The more rectangluar a cushion top, the wider an X drawn from corner to corner will be. Knowing that patchwork couldn't match that on the chair back, we added a narrow mitered border to this cushion top instead.

10 Complete the bench cushion by following steps 6 and 7 of the chair back cushion; use piece J for the boxing and piece K for the cushion bottom.

buttoned-together
cushion sham

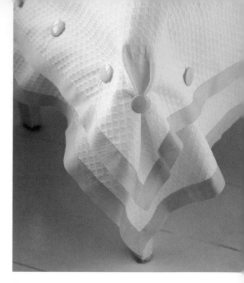

ABOUT THE SAMPLES

This sham is simply two identical pieces of fabric sandwiching a plump pillow. The layers are held together with buttons and buttonholes and the top fabric is pleated at each corner to give it dimension. The fabric is waffle-weave cotton trimmed with grosgrain ribbon. The cushion shown is about 15" wide at the front, 13" wide at the back, and 15" deep; the bottom flange extends 5" on the front and each side and 3" on the back.

MATERIALS

Fabric
Ribbon
Buttons
Thread to match
Pillow form

TECHNIQUES

Read About Cushions for Furniture, pages 88–89. Refer to Part Three, Basics, for information on making pillow forms and other sewing techniques.

MEASURE, MARK, AND CUT

Note: Referring to the diagram at right, determine the best proportions for this project: Measure the chair seat from front to back, across the front edge and across the back edge. Also determine the depth desired for the flange drop; the corners will naturally hang lower than the sides. Then refer to the directions and make a muslin template before cutting your fabric. You'll need sufficient ribbon to rim the perimeter of both layers.

(A) **SHAM TOP & BOTTOM** ✂cut 2 alike; no seam allowance is needed

PILLOW FORM

✂If you wish to use a foam form, trim the top edges and front corners to soften them, then wrap it in batting.

✂If you wish to use a soft ready-made form, use one with knife edges and follow the directions on page 112 for making a mock-boxed pillow. If your chair seat is tapered, taper the pillow by removing the excess fabric along the sides before tucking in the back corners.

SHAM

1 Centered on a piece of muslin, draft a trapezoid of the chair seat dimensions. Rule the depth desired for the flange drop around it; allow 3" across the back edge (refer to the diagram below). Cut out the muslin outside the outer line so you can adjust it on the chair.

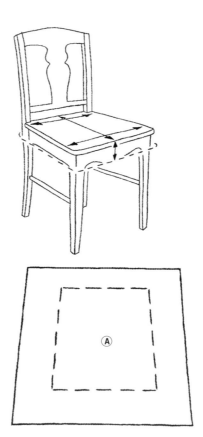

TIPS FROM THE PROS

✂If you plan to make the cushion for a backless bench or stool, extend the flange equally on all sides.

2 Place the muslin on the chair, aligning the inner outline with the seat. Put your cushion form on the seat, and check that the drop is pleasing. Refine the shape if necessary. From your fabric, cut two identical pieces this shape (A).

3 Serge or zigzag the perimeter of each sham piece. Pin grosgrain ribbon to the right side of each. Begin pinning at a back corner, positioning the ribbon so it extends slightly over the finished edge of the fabric, and folding a miter in the ribbon at each corner. Edgestitch the ribbon to the fabric; also edgestitch the fold of each miter. △

The trim tells the tale here. Whether you opt for a high-contrast or a subtle tone-on-tone finish, keep it simple or you'll lose the graphic impact.

4 Place one sham piece right side up on your worktable. Place the cushion form on top of it, with the back edge of the form about 3" from the back edge of the sham, and the front and sides evenly spaced from the sham edges. ▽

5 With the right side up, center and smooth the remaining sham piece over the form. Check that the drop extends equally on the front and sides. Pin the layers together where the top hits the tabletop, marking three evenly spaced buttonholes on each side. Fold an inverted box pleat at each corner of the top and pin across the pleats where the fabric hits the tabletop. ▽

This quirky sham adds some lighthearted padding to a hard chair. Use it at a dressing table, in a bathroom, or make a set for an informal dining area.

6 Adjust the pins so they pierce only the sham top. Remove the top. Sew across the box pleats where pinned. Make the buttonholes, placing them perpendicular to the sham edge (refer to Basics, page 121).

7 Place the top over the form and bottom again; mark the button placements. Sew a button at each mark. Button the sham top to the bottom.

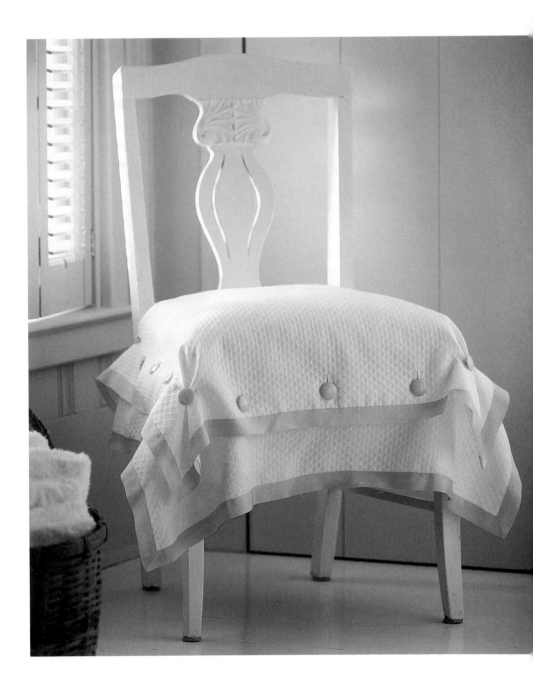

part three
basics

YOU NEED ONLY BASIC SEWING SKILLS AND A BIT OF thoughtful preparation to make a pillow. In this section you'll find general information for planning and cutting your project from your fabric, making or adapting pillow forms, and sewing. You'll also find a list of the equipment and supplies you're likely to need. Whether you are a novice or experienced sewer, review this information, as it supports and enhances the individual project directions. Also be sure to read About Knife-Edge Pillows, pages 24–25; About Square-Edge Pillows, pages 56-57; About Bolsters and Rounds, pages 72–73; and About Cushions for Furniture, pages 88–89, as appropriate.

getting started

UNDERSTANDING FABRIC

In pillow design, fabric can play the leading role. Whether you choose solid colors, an important motif, or vibrant stripes, the fabric is likely to be the first thing you notice once the pillow is done. A good understanding of fabric will help you make smart decisions as you plan your project.

Considering the Effect

Choose fabric with an appropriate weight and hand for the kind of pillow you have in mind. Consider these qualities in conjunction with the type of form you plan to use. Don't expect a soft fabric to drape or squash comfortably over a stiff foam form—or a stiff fabric to collapse invitingly over a down form.

Take advantage of the fabric design when you plan your project. Use stripes or plaids creatively; center large motifs. Design the proportions of the pillow to show off the fabric.

Anticipate construction and finishing needs from the outset. Should a sheer be backed? Should a ruffle be hemmed or cut twice as wide as needed and folded double? Will topstitching be attractive or will hand finishing look best? Answers to questions like these can affect the way you cut your project.

Understanding the Grain

The way you place the pieces of your project on the fabric when you cut them out can affect the look of the design, so take a moment to become familiar with the following terms. The **selvages** are the parallel woven edges that run the length of the fabric. The **lengthwise grain** lies parallel to the selvages. The **crosswise grain** lies perpendicular to the selvages. Both the lengthwise and crosswise grains are referred to as **straight** grains; the lengthwise grain is the most stable, the crosswise grain slightly less so. The **bias** lies at a 45-degree angle to the selvages. It is not stable, but stretches, molds, and drapes easily. Stripes and plaids cut on the bias will run diagonally. The bias can be used very effectively, but bias edges tend to stretch when they are sewn together or hemmed, so they must be handled carefully. ▽

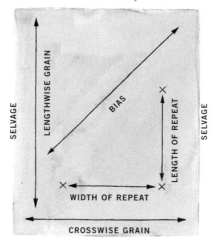

Before you can calculate the yardage, you'll have to decide which grain the pieces will be cut along. Principal pieces should be cut on the straight grain. Usually the top-to-bottom dimension of a piece is placed on the lengthwise grain. For a pillow, however, the difference between the lengthwise and crosswise grains of most fabrics is not critical unless the fabric has a directional pattern; you can probably use whichever gives the most efficient layout. Ruffles, ties, and applied bands of fabric can be cut on the straight or bias, depending upon the effect desired,

Additionally, some fabrics have repeating designs. These should be centered on each piece and matched along seamlines when appropriate. On boxed pillows, the stripes on the boxing should align at the center front with those on the top and bottom, or be cut on an opposing grain.

PLANNING SEAM ALLOWANCE

As you plan your project be sure to include seam and hem allowances in all your calculations.

✂The standard seam allowance for home decorating projects is $1/2$".

✂A hem allowance can be whatever is appropriate to the situation. If you plan to turn under the top edge of the hem, be sure to make the hem allowance deep enough to turn. If you plan to serge or zigzag the top edge, no extra hem allowance is required.

✂For an overlap closure, add three times the desired overlap to the width of the pillow back (refer to page 117).

PLANNING RUFFLE FULLNESS

How full should a gathered ruffle be? This depends upon the desired effect and the weight of the fabric. Generally, the lighter the fabric, the greater the fullness. To determine the total length of fabric needed to create the desired fullness, measure the perimeter of the pillow or the length of the seam to which the ruffle will be attached.

✂For lightweight fabrics, multiply the perimeter or length by 3.

✂For heavier fabrics, multiply the perimeter or length by $2^{1/2}$.

⚔If cutting on the crosswise grain, divide the total by the fabric width to find the number of pieces to cut.

⚔If cutting on the lengthwise grain, divide the total as necessary so you can cut economically.

⚔Don't forget to account for seam and hem allowances

TIPS FROM THE PROS

⚔The only way you can be sure of the most effective ruffle fullness is to make a small sample using your fabric.

⚔Cut ruffles generously and check their effect on the pillow; adjust as necessary.

⚔When you are calculating ruffle fullness, remember that the hem edge of the ruffle should fan attractively around the pillow corners. One way to ensure that it does is to concentrate the gathers at the corners when you apply the ruffle; you might also want to allow some extra fullness.

UNDERSTANDING BIAS STRIPS

Because it stretches, is flexible, and curves nicely, true bias, which falls on a 45-degree angle between the lengthwise and crosswise grainlines, should be used to cover welting or bind project edges.

Bias strips can be used as a single layer or folded in half lengthwise and then sewn as though the two layers were one (called double, or French fold, bias; refer to pages 118–19 for more information). If your binding/piping fabric is sheer, use double bias—it will be opaque. To determine the width to cut a bias strip, first calculate the width the strip should be when finished.

⚔For welting, the finished width is the amount needed to wrap around the cording; add twice the seam allowance to this dimension to find the cut width. If you wish to cover the cord with a double layer of fabric, cut the bias strip twice as wide as for a single layer.

⚔For binding, the finished width is the amount of binding you wish to show on the right side along the edge of the project. Binding is easiest to apply when its seam allowance is equal to its finished width. For single binding, shown below, quadruple the finished width to find the cut width. For French fold binding, multiply the finished width by six to find the cut width. ▽

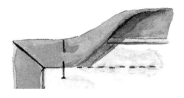

TIPS FROM THE PROS

⚔If binding heavy fabric or multiple layers, add about $1/8$" to the cut width of the binding so it will turn comfortably over the project edge.

Planning for Bias Strips

To minimize bulky seams, try to cut the longest possible bias strips; it's worth the results to invest in a little extra fabric. Here are some guidelines for planning the longest bias you can cut from some commonly encountered amounts of fabric:

⚔from $1/2$ yard any width fabric: 25"

⚔from 1 yard any width fabric: 50"

⚔from a piece 44" x 44": 62"

⚔from a piece 52" x 52": 73"

Cutting Bias Strips

To find the bias, place one leg of a 45-degree right-angle triangle on the selvage and mark along the hypotenuse, or fold the fabric diagonally so the crosswise threads are parallel to the selvage and mark the fold. You can mark and cut the strips individually, but here is an efficient way to cut large quantities.

Mark the longest possible bias line on your fabric and cut along it. Beginning at one 45-degree corner, fold the fabric repeatedly, aligning the bias edge. Mark strips of the desired width parallel to the bias edge and cut through all layers—pin first to keep the layers aligned. (If you use a rotary cutter and transparent ruler, you won't have to mark the strips or pin the layers.) ▽

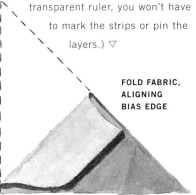

FOLD FABRIC, ALIGNING BIAS EDGE

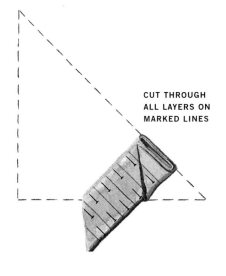

CUT THROUGH ALL LAYERS ON MARKED LINES

REVIEWING YOUR MATH

When you're planning your project, you may need to draft some pattern pieces. Here are some reminders of the basic rules for common geometric shapes.

Right Triangles

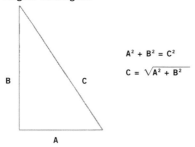

$$A^2 + B^2 = C^2$$
$$C = \sqrt{A^2 + B^2}$$

Circles

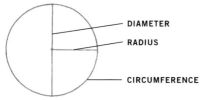

DIAMETER
RADIUS
CIRCUMFERENCE

RADIUS = DIAMETER ÷ 2

CIRCUMFERENCE = DIAMETER X 3.1415

Drafting Circles

Small circles can be drafted with a compass. To draft a large circle, first put the fabric or paper on a board or cutting mat you can pin into. Tie a piece of string around a sharp pencil. On the string, measure the desired radius of the circle from the pencil, add $1/2$" for seam allowance, and place a pin through the string at this point; pin through the fabric or paper into the board or mat beneath. Hold the pencil upright, pull the string taut, and draw a circle. ▽

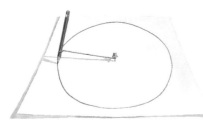

CALCULATING YARDAGE

Because most pillows have just a few pieces, and those pieces are as often as not either square or rectangular, it's almost always quite simple to figure out how much fabric will be required. For each design, you need simply to know how many pieces there are, the dimensions of each, and the width of the fabric or fabrics you'll be using. In most cases, you can make your yardage calculations from a list and sketch; for a very complex project, you might want to make a scale layout on graph paper.

Analyzing the Design

To begin, analyze the design you plan to make and determine how many pieces are involved and how many fabrics you wish to use. If you are making one of the projects in this book, we've listed and drawn the pieces for you. However, you may want to use more or fewer fabrics than are shown in the photos. If you are making a design of your own, follow our example to sketch and label the component pieces.

✂ If you will be making a pillow form with loose stuffing, follow the steps below and use the desired dimensions to calcuate the muslin yardage.

Sketching the Components

It's easiest to visualize the fabric requirements if you sketch the component pieces in relation to the way they'll be assembled, as we have done for each project in this book. Make your sketch roughly proportional—it doesn't have to be perfect. Include foldlines, hem allowances, or other details, so you don't forget to allow for them. If your design calls for more than one fabric,

use colored pencils to differentiate them on your sketch. Jot the dimensions of each piece (measure the pillow form) on the sketch or on a separate list and note the number to cut of each. Include the seam allowance ($1/2$" all around) when noting the dimensions. Here, for example, is our plan for the French-Cuff Pillow Slip shown on pages 38–39. ▽

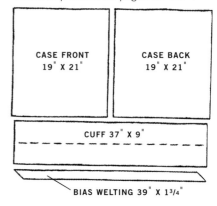

CASE FRONT 19" X 21"

CASE BACK 19" X 21"

CUFF 37" X 9"

BIAS WELTING 39" X 1 3/4"

You can see that this project has three components, of which one must be cut twice. You could cut all the pieces from one fabric or cut each from a different fabric as we did. As another option, you could cut the front, back, and cuff from one fabric and the welting from another, as shown on page 59, where we turned the cuff perpendicular to the case to take advantage of the stripe.

TIPS FROM THE PROS

✂ The fabrics you choose and the way you use them affect not only the look of the finished project, but also the amount of material you'll need. If you know which fabrics you'll use from the start, you can make an accurate yardage calculation. If you don't, make an estimate and adjust it when you're shopping.

Making a Paper Pattern

In pillow making there is very little need for paper patterns, as most of the pieces are geometric and can be drawn directly on the fabric. However, there are times when you may find it useful to work out a shape or detail on paper. And some people simply prefer to use a paper pattern as a cutting guide.

To make a pattern, draft the shape of each piece on paper. Rule the seam allowance all around. If the straight grain is not parallel to one edge, mark the grainline; also mark any match points. Cut out each piece.

✂ If you are making cushions for furniture, place muslin or paper over the seat (and back, if appropriate) and make a template of the shape.

✂ If you wish to make multiples of a pillow, do make paper patterns—they'll save time in the long run.

TIPS FROM THE PROS

✂ If all the pieces of your pillow are square or rectangular, you can include the seam allowance in the dimensions when you draft the pattern.

✂ If the pieces of your pillow are not all square or rectangular, draft them all before adding seam allowance to any. Measure all the corresponding edges to be sure they match, then rule on the seam allowance.

Trueing up a pattern: To true up a pattern, first fold the pattern in half, lengthwise or widthwise, as appropriate. To check the outline for symmetry, use dressmaker's tracing paper and a tracing wheel to transfer the marks from one half to the other. If the transferred

marks don't align with the drawn marks, draw a new line in between them. Cut out the pattern on the new line, adding seam allowance first if appropriate.

Making a Cutting Layout

Once you've determined the way you want to align the pieces on your fabric, sketch the cutting layout; note the width of the fabric and the dimensions of the pieces on the sketch. If you wish, you can make a scale drawing, but because you're probably not dealing with many pieces, a sketch should suffice—just check that the combined width of adjacent pieces doesn't exceed the fabric width. Make a sketch for each fabric you plan to use. Shown are layouts for cutting the French-Cuff Pillow Slip from one fabric and from three; in both cases the fabrics are 45" wide. ▽

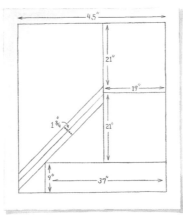

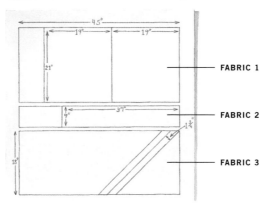

Determining the Yardage

To determine how much fabric you'll need, add together the lengthwise dimensions of the pieces on your layout sketch. Divide the total by 36, the number of inches in a yard.

PREPARING THE FABRIC

If you plan to wash your pillow cover, preshrink the fabric before cutting by washing and drying it in the method you will use in the future. To ensure accurate cutting, always press the fabric first so it will lie flat and wrinkle-free on your cutting table. If the selvages are woven tighter than the rest of the fabric, cut them off.

CUTTING

Place the fabric wrong side up on your cutting table. (If the fabric has a repeating pattern that is not visible on the wrong side, place the fabric right side up.) Arrange the pillow pieces on the fabric according to your sketch; draft them using rulers and chalk as you go, or use patterns if you prepared them. Center, match, or align any fabric pattern as planned. Cut out the pieces. Transfer any match points to the pieces.

about pillow forms

There are two principal types of pillow forms: filled cloth and foam. Both are so widely available at home and fabric stores that it is hardly worth the trouble to make a form unless you can't find the size you require.

FILLED CLOTH FORMS

Cloth forms can be filled with loose polyester stuffing or with feathers and/or down. Polyester-filled pillows range in quality from firm to fairly soft. Down-and-feather-filled pillows are soft and squishy. If you want your pillow form to relax when it's handled, opt for down-and-feather filling; even the softest polyester stuffing springs back into shape when pressure is released. As explained at right, ready-made forms can be altered if they're not exactly the size you need.

✂ For best results when making a filled form, purchase good-quality polyester stuffing; make sure it shreds easily and can be manipulated without forming lumps. The covering can be muslin or any similar fabric.

✂ Down-and-feather filled forms should be professionally made. This is especially true for large cushions, which should have interior channels to keep the filling evenly distributed. The covering must be downproof.

Making a Filled Form

Cut and sew the cover for the form exactly as you would the finished pillow, omitting any welting or trims and leaving a 6" opening in the seam on one edge. Stuff the cover; it is not necessary to turn it right side out first. Sew the opening closed by hand or machine.

Cutting Down a Filled Form

If you are making a knife-edge pillow and can't find a form in the size you need, buy one that is larger. Open the seam along one edge and remove some of the stuffing. Push the remaining stuffing toward the opposite edge and pin off the excess fabric. Sew the cover closed along the pin line, then trim off the excess fabric. Pin and sew along two adjacent edges if both dimensions of the form are too large.

Making a Mock-Boxed Pillow

Ready-made boxed pillow forms are not always readily available, but it's easy to alter a knife-edge form to give it a boxed shape. To judge the size with which to start, add the desired thickness to both the desired width and the desired length. For example, for a 12"-wide x 15"-long x 3"-thick mock-boxed form, begin with a 15" x 18" knife-edge form.

✂ To create a form with crisp corners, grasp the cover at one corner and push the filling toward the center, aligning the adjacent perimeter seams to form a point. Pin and sew across the point as shown. The length of this seam will establish the thickness of the form: the further it lies from the point, the thicker the form will be. Repeat at each corner, then trim the excess fabric close to the seams. ▽

✂ To create a form with soft, rounded corners, push one corner point into the pillow form, forming a tuck perpendicular to the perimeter seam; tack the edges of the tuck together at the seamline. The length of the tuck will establish the thickness of the form: the further it lies from the point, the thicker the form will be. Repeat at each corner. ▽

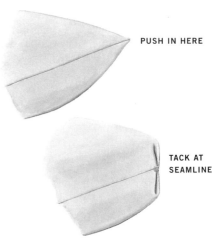

PUSH IN HERE

TACK AT SEAMLINE

FOAM FORMS

Foam forms are available ready-made in a variety of sizes and shapes; many vendors will cut them to order. Foam forms are quite rigid.

✂ Should you need to cut your own form, use an electric knife. If you are trimming a small amount and don't need a perfectly clean cut, you can use a utility knife.

✂ If necessary, use spray glue to adhere two pieces of foam.

Softening the Look of Foam Forms

To soften the look of a foam form, wrap it in one or more layers of polyester batting. Use spray glue to adhere the batting to the foam, trim the batting so the edges butt rather than overlap, then spray glue along the edges and press them together.

You'll use a variety of sewing techniques as you make your pillows. If you are an experienced sewer, you'll see that making a pillow does not differ greatly from making apparel. Whatever your skill level, take the time to review the following information, as some techniques may be unfamiliar to you.

PRESSING

Pressing during each stage of construction will result in a good-looking project that requires only a light touch-up when completed. After sewing a seam, press the seam flat to meld the stitches and then, in most cases, press the seam allowance open.

TIPS FROM THE PROS

✂ To avoid creating creases when pressing pillow covers, slide the area to be pressed over a sleeve board.

✂ If seams are bulky and turned together in one direction, grade (trim) each layer to a different width. Generally, the seam allowance closest to the top fabric is left widest. Grading helps seams lie flat without bulk so they don't appear as unsightly ridges on the right side of your project.

HAND-SEWING TECHNIQUES

Hand sewing is used for temporary stitching or for finishing. Use a single, rather than double, strand of thread and wax it for better control. For temporary stitching, do not knot the thread; secure it with a couple of small stitches instead. This assures that you'll cut the thread to free it before pulling it out—pulling forgotten knots through the fabric can leave holes or otherwise mar its surface.

Blindstitch

The blindstitch is used for hemming and holding facings in place, and is inconspicuous on both sides. First, finish the cut edge of the hem or facing. Roll this edge back about $1/4$". Work from right to left. Make a small horizontal stitch under one thread of the fabric, then under a thread of the hem or facing diagonally opposite the first stitch. ▽

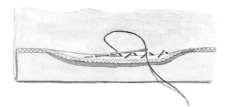

Running Stitch

The running stitch is a temporary stitch used for basting seams to secure their alignment during construction and for gathering or easing during pin fitting. Space stitches evenly, $1/4$" long and $1/4$" apart. If basting to align a pattern, be precise, inserting the needle perpendicularly through all layers and checking as you work. ▽

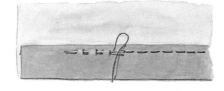

Stab Stitch

The stab stitch is a precise and nearly invisible stitch used to secure and align one layer to another. It is especially good for sewing on trims that would be crushed by a sewing machine. Inserting the needle straight up and down through the layers, make very short stitches; the stitches can be longer on the wrong side than on the right side.

Slipstitch

The slipstitch provides an almost invisible finish for hems, linings, and trims. Working from right to left, insert the needle into the folded edge of the upper layer, slide it inside the fold, bring it out about $1/8$"–$1/4$" from the insertion point, then slide the needle under a single thread of the lower layer. Repeat. When slipstitching braids or other trims, slide the needle through and along the woven or twisted edge, concealing the thread. ▽

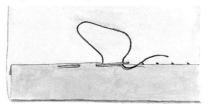

MACHINE-SEWING TECHNIQUES

The directions in this book call for a variety of machine stitches and seams. These are explained below, along with some others that you may find useful.

Baste

To sew with temporary stitches, either to hold pieces together so you can check the fit or to secure two layers to which a third will be added, as when inserting welting. Basting allows you to accurately align seams. Use the longest stitch setting. If you are matching pieces prior to making permanent seams, sew on the seamline. If you are holding multiple layers together so they can be treated as one, sew in the seam allowance.

Staystitch

To reinforce a seamline before sewing one piece of fabric to another, usually so that the seam allowance can be clipped and spread without risk of tearing. Generally, staystitching is done through one layer of fabric with a short straight stitch.

Edgestitch

To secure a folded edge to another layer of fabric by topstitching through all layers as close to the fold as possible.

Topstitch

To stitch through one or more layers with the project right side up in the machine. Topstitching can be decorative or functional or both. Use a thread color and stitch length that are appropriate to the situation.

Finish the Edge

For durability, the cut edge of seam allowances should not be left raw. In general, you should finish the edges as you work, selecting a method that is appropriate for your fabric and equipment—zigzag, serge, fold-and-topstitch are three common options. In this book, the direction to "finish the edges" is given as a reminder only when we felt it would be difficult to accomplish at a later stage.

Gather

To draw up a length of fabric with stitches, as when making a ruffle. Gathers can be adjustable, so you can manipulate and distribute the fullness as desired. If you have a ruffler foot or attachment, they can be stitched to a set tension; these will be even

but cannot be tightened or loosened, so refer to the attachment manual and make a test piece.

✄For basted adjustable gathers, make two parallel rows of basting stitches, one on the seamline, one just inside the seam allowance. Pull the bobbin threads to gather the fabric to the desired fullness; wrap them in a figure eight around a pin to secure temporarily. ▽

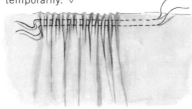

✄For zigzag adjustable gathers, lay button thread or monofilament over the seamline and zigzag stitch over it. Pull the button thread to gather the fabric to the desired fullness; wrap it in a figure eight around a pin to secure temporarily. ▽

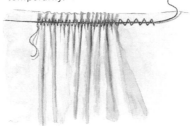

TIPS FROM THE PROS

✄When gathering long pieces, make several short runs of gathering stitches—they're easier to pull up without breaking. First divide the edge to be gathered into logical segments—for instance, quarter it to apportion to each side of a square pillow.

Serged Seam

A serger produces an overlocking stitch to prevent raveling as it trims excess fabric from the seam allowance. A three-thread stitch formation is commonly used as an edge finish. A four-thread stitch formation can seam and finish in one pass.

Zigzag Seam

A sturdy, ravel-proof seam. Place the fabric right sides together. Stitch on the seamline, using a narrow, short zigzag 1mm wide and 1mm long. In the seam allowance, stitch again, using a zigzag 2mm wide and 2mm long. Trim the excess seam allowance.

French Seam

An enclosed seam well suited to straight seams on sheer fabric. Allow $5/8$" seam allowance when cutting. With fabric wrong sides together, stitch a plain seam $3/8$" from the seamline in the seam allowance. Trim to $1/8$" from stitching. Press the seam to one side. Fold along the stitched seam, bringing the right sides of the fabric together, and press. Stitch along the seamline, encasing the raw edges. ▽

HEMS

Hems can be made by hand or machine, as you wish, although in pillow making, there is generally little reason to hem by hand. Because sewing equipment and fabric choice play a part in choosing the best hem method, the directions in this book do not always recommend a specific technique. Refer to page 108 for information about adding hem allowance. Refer to hand-sewing techniques, page 113, and machine-sewing techniques, pages 113–14, for specific stitches.

Stitch-Turn-Stitch Baby Hem

A delicate, completely finished hem for sheers and lightweight fabrics. Stitch through one layer of fabric in the seam allowance 1/8" from the hemline. Press the fabric to the wrong side along the stitching line, then stitch close to the folded edge. On the wrong side, carefully trim the excess fabric close to the stitching. Press the fabric to the wrong side along this stitching line, and stitch again next to the new fold. ▽

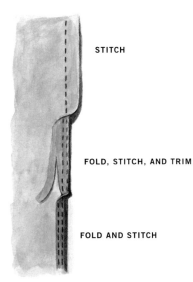

STITCH

FOLD, STITCH, AND TRIM

FOLD AND STITCH

Rolled Hem

Rolled hems are narrow, softly rolled edges created with a special rolled hem attachment or adjustment on a serger or with a special presser foot on a sewing machine. They are commonly used on sheers and lightweight fabrics. Make a test to determine the appropriate seam allowance and stitch length for your fabric.

TIPS FROM THE PROS

✂ A quick rolled hem can be made on a lightweight or sheer fabric by folding the fabric to the wrong side and stitching with a narrow, short zigzag stitch, 1mm wide and 1mm long, on the folded edge. On the wrong side, carefully trim the excess fabric close to the stitching.

RUFFLES

A ruffle can be a single layer of fabric or one that is folded double. A folded ruffle looks equally attractive on the front and back; it requires less finishing because the fold serves as a hem.
✂ Ruffles cut on the straight grain tend to be crisp, while those cut on the bias drape softly, but the hand of the fabric also affects this. Additionally, directional fabrics, such as stripes, checks, and plaids, have different effects when run vertically, horizontally, or diagonally.
✂ Two ruffles can be applied one on top of the other; these can be the same or different depths. If the fabrics are lightweight, you can gather the two ruffles together. If the fabrics are heavier, gather the ruffles separately and then baste them together to keep them aligned while you sew them to the project.

Attaching a Ruffle

When a strip of fabric is made into a ruffle, gathers or pleats are secured a short distance from one edge. The area above the gathers is called a header.
✂ If the header edge is finished with a hem or trim, the ruffle is applied on top of the project so the header adds a flourish; it can be any depth that seems pleasing. Applied ruffles can usually be topstitched to a project by machine. ▽

✂ If the header edge is left raw, the ruffle must be inserted in a seam. In this case, the header should be the depth of the seam allowance used throughout the project. When you are ready to attach the ruffle, pin it to the project with right sides together and cut edges aligned. Welting or other trim can be inserted between the ruffle and the project. ▽

TIPS FROM THE PROS

✂ Gathers can be bulky. Be sure your machine can handle all the layers before you insert multiple layers of ruffles and welting in a seam.

construction techniques

SEWING CORNERS AND CURVES

When joining a straight edge to a corner or curve, you will have to clip the seam allowance of one piece or the other so the layers will lie flat while you sew the seam. You'll encounter this situation whenever you are sewing boxing to a pillow or the ends onto a bolster.

If you have never sewn these seams, test the techniques using muslin or scraps of your fabric.

Outside Corners

To turn a corner when attaching a straight piece, such as a boxing band or welting, pin the band to the other piece of fabric above the corner, right sides together and cut edges aligned. At the corner, clip the seam allowance of the band only right up to the seamline, pivot the band around the corner, and continue pinning. ▽

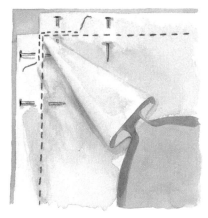

TIPS FROM THE PROS

✂ If there is a seam in the straight piece where it meets the corner, don't clip, just remove the stitches from the end of the seam.

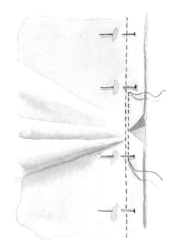

Inside Corners

To attach a straight piece, such as a boxing band or welting, to an inside corner, first staystitch the corner along the seamline and clip the corner seam allowance right up to the stitches. Pin the piece with the corner to the band, right sides together and cut edges aligned, spreading the fabric to fit the band. △

Outside Curves

To attach a straight piece, such as a boxing band or welting, to an outside curve, pin the straight piece to the curved piece, right sides together and cut edges aligned. At the curve, clip the seam allowance of the band only right up to the seamline, clipping only as needed to spread the seam allowance around the curve. ▽

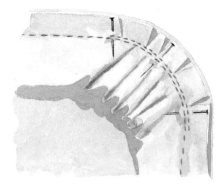

Inside Curves

To attach a straight piece, such as a boxing band or welting, to an inside curve, first staystitch the curved section along the seamline. Pin the piece with the curve to the band, right sides together and cut edges aligned. Clip the seam allowance of the curve right up to the staystitching, clipping only as needed to spread the fabric to fit the band. ▽

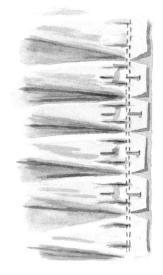

TIPS FROM THE PROS

✂ Before clipping into a seam allowance, staystitch the seamline to reinforce it.

✂ When attaching a straight band to a piece that has both inside and outside corners or curves, place pins on both sides of the seam. Hand baste these sections before sewing so you won't have to pull pins out from the underside as they reach the needle.

✂ When inserting welting between two pieces of a pillow, sew it to the right side of one piece along the seamline before topping with the second piece.

MAKING AN OVERLAP CLOSURE

An overlap closure permits easy removal of a pillow cover. Pillow covers made with overlap closures are often called shams.

To set up an overlap closure, cut the pillow back or bottom in two sections. Along the adjacent edges, add an underlap allowance to one section and a hem allowance to both sections; the underlap and hem allowances should be equal. For most pillows, a 1½" underlap is good, so add 3" to the finished width of one section, 1½" to the other. If you plan to turn under the cut edge of the hem, add an additional ½"; if you plan to serge or zigzag it, no additional allowance is required. ▽

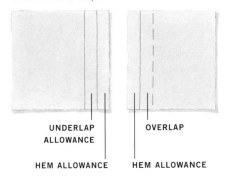

UNDERLAP ALLOWANCE   OVERLAP

HEM ALLOWANCE   HEM ALLOWANCE

The easiest way to prepare an overlap closure is by cutting the back sections a bit wider than you actually need them, making the hems, overlapping the sections, and then trimming any excess so the pillow back is exactly the size of the front. This gives you a bit of flexibility should the hems not come out exactly as anticipated, or should you wish to increase the lap to cover the stitching or perfect the pattern alignment.

TIPS FROM THE PROS

✄ If your fabric is a solid or has a small pattern, cut the pillow back in one piece, making it about 6" wider than needed. Then cut it into two sections.

✄ If your fabric has a pattern or motif that should be matched along the overlap, plan ahead. Cut each section of the back separately, adding the allowances beyond the match line. Be sure to cut a right and a left piece.

✄ The overlap can be centered on the pillow or set off-center. If you fasten the overlap with buttons or ties, the pillow back could be as attractive as the front.

✄ If you wish to close the overlap with ties, cut the hem of the underlap section extra deep so it will support the ties—they'll be sewn next to the overlap edge, not on the underlap allowance. ▽

Sewing an Overlap Closure

1 Press the hem allowance to the wrong side of each section of the pillow back along the overlap edge. Finish the inside edge of each hem, then stitch each hem. ▽

2 Place the pillow backs right side up and overlap the hemmed edges; pin to hold temporarily. Center the pillow front on the backs; pin. Trim any excess fabric from the pillow back. ▽

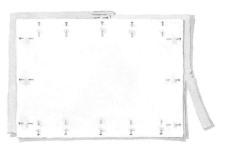

3 Separate all the pieces. If desired, make buttonholes in the hem of the overlapping back (refer to page 121) or sew corresponding pieces of hook-and-loop tape to the inside of one hem and the outside of the other.

✄ If using ties, pin them in position while the back sections are lapped; then separate the back sections and sew on the ties.

4 Place the sham backs right side up and overlap the hemmed edges; be sure the appropriate one is on top. Pin them together at each end of the overlap. If you wish, baste the hem ends together so they remain aligned while you finish the pillow cover.

5 Proceed with the directions for making your pillow.

USING TRIMS

Trims dress up a pillow. They take more stress from everyday use than you might anticipate, so select varieties that appear durable. Whether you make or purchase your trims, preshrink them if appropriate.

Joining Bias Strips

Press-stretch bias strips before working with them for easier handling and smoother results. Before joining the strips, check to see that their ends are on the straight grain; recut if necessary. Place two strips right sides together, with the ends aligned as shown, and sew together. Repeat to join all the strips, then press all the seam allowances open. ▽

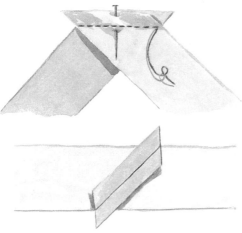

TIPS FROM THE PROS

✂When piecing striped, napped, or otherwise directionally patterned bias strips, check to be sure that the pattern or nap is always facing the same way— you may have to recut the ends of the strips (to the opposite straight grain) to maintain the alignment.

Welting/Piping

To make welting/piping, put a zipper or piping foot on your machine, aligning it to the left of the needle. Center cable cord on the wrong side of a bias strip. Fold the strip over the cord, aligning cut edges—there is no need to pin. Feed the cord and bias into the machine with the cord to the right of the needle, the seam allowance to the left, under the foot. Stitch close to the cord, continuing to fold the bias over the cord as you sew. Trim the seam allowances to an even $1/2$". ▽

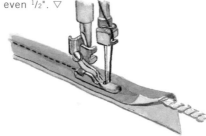

To attach welting/piping, pin it to the right side of the pillow section, aligning the cut edges. Position the zipper or piping foot to the right of your needle, and feed the piece into the machine, welting side up, with the cord to the left of the needle and the seam allowance to the right, under the foot. Stitch over the previous stitching on the welting. ▽

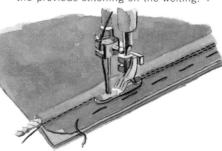

TIPS FROM THE PROS

✂Use French fold bias when working with sheer fabrics—it will be self-lined and mask the cord or fabric it covers.

To attach another piece of fabric, such as a boxing strip, place the two pieces right sides together, with the wrong side of the welted piece facing up. Align the cut edges and pin along the previous line of stitching. Move the needle position closer to the welting and stitch right next to the previous stitching.

To end welting at a seam or edge, stop stitching just before the intersecting seamline. Push the bias casing back and trim the inner cord. Pull the bias back over the cord, swing the folded edge of the welting across the seamline, and stitch over it. ▽

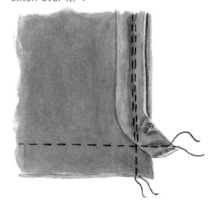

Joining welting ends: When welting ends must butt (as when rimming a cushion), place the join at the center of the least conspicuous edge, not at a corner. Leave both ends of the welting free for about 1", then overlap them and cut the excess from the finishing end about 1" beyond the starting end. Remove the stitching that secures the bias over the cord from the finishing end, and cut the cord so it butts the starting end. Fold up the end of the extending bias and place the starting end of the welting on it. Wrap the bias over the joint and complete the seam. ▽

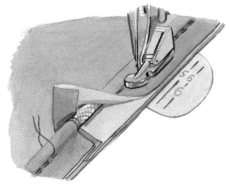

✂If your fabric is heavy, overlap and trim the welting about 2" beyond the starting end, then trim and fold up the extending bias diagonally, on the straight grain. The folded edge will wrap diagonally over the butting cords, creating less bulk than a fold placed perpendicular to the seam. ▽

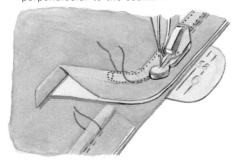

Single and Double Binding

Binding encloses an edge without adding or subtracting dimension, so cut the edge you plan to bind on its finished line—trim any seam or hem allowance before applying the binding. The bias strips used for binding can be applied single or double.

When binding is applied double, it is sometimes called French fold binding. French fold binding is a good choice for lightweight fabrics. It is faster to apply because the edge that is turned to the inside of the project is already folded and ready to hem.

Applying Single Binding

1 Press the binding strip in half lengthwise, right side out. Unfold the binding and press the cut edges to the center creaseline. ▽

2 Unfold the binding on one edge. With right sides together and cut edges aligned, pin the binding to the edge of the project. Stitch along the creaseline. ▽

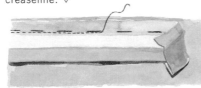

3 Fold the binding to the wrong side of the project, encasing the cut edge. On the wrong side, align the folded edge of the binding with the line of stitching. Pin and slipstitch. ▽

4 If the ends of the binding will be covered by an adjacent seam, leave them unfinished. If an end requires finishing, fold up the seam allowance before sewing the binding to the project. To join the ends of the binding, fold one end up and lap the other end over it, then sew through all layers. ▽

Applying Double Binding

1 Press the binding strip in half lengthwise, right side out.

2 With right sides together and cut edges aligned, pin the binding to the edge of the project. Stitch together, placing the seam one-third of the folded strip's width from the edge.

To complete the binding, follow steps 3 and 4 for Single Binding, left.

TIPS FROM THE PROS

✂French fold binding can be machine stitched to the wrong side of the project when it has been cut slightly wider than needed. Apply and fold it over the edge in the usual manner; the folded edge of the binding will extend beyond the stitching line. Pin, and on the right side of the project, stitch in the ditch of the seam through all layers.

construction techniques

Purchased Trims

Purchased trims, such as decorator welting or piping, cord, braid, and fringe, add a professional touch to a pillow. Many styles ravel when cut, and finishing their ends can be awkward. Use care and common sense when working with them, keeping the cut ends wrapped with tape until ready for the final finishing. Sew decorator welting to your project as you do fabric-covered welting (see page 118). Cord must be sewn on by hand. Braid and fringe can be sewn on by hand or machine, depending upon the type and the intended use. If possible, finish trim ends by turning them under or concealing in an adjacent seam. Otherwise, use a fray retardant or bind with small stitches.

TIPS FROM THE PROS

✄The terms *welting* and *piping* are used interchangeably by most people. They refer to round trim that has a flange seam allowance, which is sewn into the seams of the pillow. Welting/piping can be fabric covered or made of decorative twisted cords sewn to a cloth tape.
✄The terms *cord* or *cording* refer to a cord that has no flange. Cable cord is the cord used inside fabric-covered welting/piping.

Attaching fringe: Fringe is held together with stitches along one edge. This area is called a header.
✄To conceal the header in a seam, place the fringe and one pillow piece right sides together, aligning the lower edge of the header with the seamline of the pillow piece; sew the header to the pillow piece seam allowance. Clip the header at corners as necessary.

✄Some headers are attractive, and you can stitch them on top of your project if you like the effect. It's usually easiest to do this by hand after the pillow cover is assembled. Fold miters into the header at corners as necessary.

Joining twisted-cord piping ends:
When twisted-cord piping ends must butt (as when rimming a cushion), place the join at the center of the least conspicuous edge. Snip the stitches that hold the cord to the tape flange, freeing about 1½" at each end. Overlap the ends of the tape, folding up the bottom one behind the top one. Wrap the cord ends together in consecutive order, overlapping them on the tape. Staystitch the cords to the tape. ▽

FASTENINGS

Fastenings can be discreetly concealed or visible and decorative. A pillow cover that will be laundered should be easy to remove and resecure. Choose fastenings that are compatible with the weight of the pillow cover fabric.

Ties

To construct a simple narrow tie, cut a strip of fabric on the straight grain, making it four times the finished width of the tie and long enough to make one or more ties; include seam allowance in the length. Fold the strip in half lengthwise, right side out, and press. Open out the strip, then fold each long edge to the center creaseline; press.

Fold the strip in half lengthwise and press again. Cut the strip into pieces of the appropriate length. Topstitch each tie closed, first turning in the seam allowance at one or both ends, as needed. (If one end of the tie will be inserted in a seam, leave the end unfinished.) ▽

Slot Zipper

Install centered on a plain seam, as on the back boxing strip of a cushion. Sew the seam, basting the portion where the zipper will go, and press it open. Center the zipper, right side down, over the seam allowance, and baste. Using a zipper foot, topstitch ⅜" from each side of the seamline, sewing across the tape at the closed end of the zipper. ▽

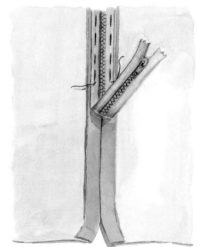

Piped or Welted Zipper

Install on a piped seam, as on the perimeter seam of a dart-shaped pillow. The welting masks the zipper. Sew the seam, leaving open the portion where the zipper will go. Press under the seam allowance in the open area. Open the zipper and position it so the welting just covers the zipper teeth. (Be sure the open end of the zipper is at the open end of the seam, if there is one.) With a zipper foot, stitch in the ditch of the welting seam through all layers. Close the zipper. Align the opposite (folded) edge of the open seam with the piping seamline, covering the zipper teeth; baste the zipper in place. Open the zipper and stitch $1/8$" from the teeth. ▽

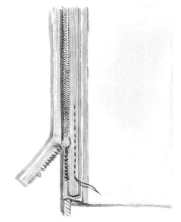

Buttons

Buttons can be of the sew-through or shank variety. Covered buttons almost always have a shank.

✂ To attach a sew-through button, wax a strand of thread, place it in a needle, and knot it. Insert the needle and thread from the wrong side of the fabric up through one hole in the button. Place a toothpick across the button between the holes. Take several stitches through the holes, making the stitches parallel to the corresponding buttonhole. Bring the needle and thread out between the button and fabric. Remove the toothpick; lift the button away from the fabric so the stitches are tight against the button. Wind the thread around the stitches several times to form a shank. Secure the thread on the right side with several small stitches close to the shank. △

✂ To attach a shank button, begin as described above and simply pass the needle several times through the fabric and the eye of the shank. Finish by knotting the thread on the wrong side of the fabric or by making several small stitches close to the shank.

TIPS FROM THE PROS

✂ When sewing buttons to thin or loosely woven fabric, reinforce the point of attachment by placing a small, flat button on the wrong side of the fabric. Stitch through both buttons and form a shank under the functional button as described above.

✂ You can use a piece of interfacing in place of the second button. For sheers, use a piece of the same fabric.

Buttonholes

The size of a buttonhole should always be determined by the size of the button. Minimum buttonhole length should equal the diameter plus the thickness of the button plus an additional $1/8$" to allow for the shank and a slight size reduction due to fabric thickness. Machine buttonholes should be made through at least two layers of fabric. Often a piece of interfacing or a third layer of fabric should be added. Always test the buttonhole on a scrap of your fabric.

TIPS FROM THE PROS

✂ Buttonholes can be an important part of a pillow's design. Consider stitching them with contrasting thread or, if you are an experienced sewer, give a tailored look to a closure by making bound buttonholes.

Hook-and-Loop Tape

Suitable for securing lapped openings. Hook-and-loop tape (Velcro™) is available in coin shapes, small squares, small fastener strips, and by the yard in $5/8$", $3/4$", $1^1/_2$", and 2" widths. To apply, straight-stitch along each outer edge. The tape has no bias, so it tends to stiffen closures. The small pieces are handy for securing overlap closures.

TIPS FROM THE PROS

✂ Hook-and-loop tape can snag fabrics—avoid using it on damask, loosely woven textures, and velvet.

essential equipment

Probably the most important aid you need for pillow making, aside from a reasonably sturdy sewing machine, is a well-lit workspace. However, there are many tools and materials that smooth the sewing process. While some of these are common household items, you'll find that items designed for specific tasks save time and give professional results. Most of these are available at fabric or art supply stores. If you have trouble locating something, refer to the ads in a sewing magazine for a mail-order vendor.

FOR MEASURING AND MARKING

You'll need measuring and marking aids when you are planning your project, making patterns, and marking cutting and seam lines. Having a variety of these items ensures accuracy and saves time.

Tape Measure

A flexible cloth or fiberglass tape, $1/2$" x 60", is essential for taking measurements around pillow forms and on furniture. Look for one that is marked on both sides, with the numeral 1 at opposite ends.

Yardsticks and Rulers

Use a yardstick to measure fabric width and yardage. Use a yardstick or ruler as a measuring guide and straightedge when marking cutting lines on fabric.
✂Wooden yardsticks (1" x 36") are readily available; check for warping if using as a straightedge.
✂An assortment of metal and plastic rulers is indispensable—6", 12", 24", and 48" lengths are most useful. The clear, grid-printed plastic variety is handy when ruling on seam allowance.

T-Square and L-Square

Squares are useful for measuring 45- and 90-degree angles and for finding and marking the lengthwise, crosswise, or bias grain on fabric. They can be made of metal or plastic.

45-degree Right-Angle Triangles

Made of clear plastic and available in many sizes, these are especially useful for finding and marking fabric bias and mitered seams.

TIPS FROM THE PROS

✂Purchase metal rulers, squares, and triangles at fabric, quilting, or art supply stores, where they are available in lightweight aluminum that slides easily over fabric on the cutting table. The carpenter's rulers available in home and hardware stores are too heavy.

Seam Gauge

This is a small metal ruler with a sliding marker. It's great for marking seam and hem lines and for checking smaller measurements during construction.

Pencil

Use pencils to mark clear, long-lasting seam and cutting lines and match marks. If the fabric will be laundered, a regular lead pencil is a good marker. Erasable pencil markers in a variety of colors are available in fabric stores.

Dressmaker's Chalk

Use chalk to make temporary marks (seamlines, pleats, match marks). Because dressmaker's chalk can be brushed off after use, markings can be made on the right side of the fabric.

✂Available in block or pencil form, chalks come in a variety of colors.
✂Also available is a refillable powdered chalk dispenser with a wheel marker that makes crisp lines—it's great used along a ruler.

Transfer Paper and Tracing Wheels

These are found in all fabric stores. Use them to quickly transfer seamlines and match marks to multiple pieces. One side of the paper is coated with a waxy transfer medium. A path traced by a wheel run over the wrong side of the paper will transfer marks to whatever faces the right side, so place the paper between pattern and fabric or between layers of fabric, as needed.
✂The paper comes packaged in a mix of colors; some notions stores carry large (2' x 3') sheets. Not all transfer paper marks wash out, so test on a scrap, try to use on the wrong side of the fabric, and be very careful using on sheers.
✂Tracing wheels come with smooth, serrated, or needlepoint edges. The smooth edge leaves a solid line; the serrated, a closely spaced dotted line. The needlepoint leaves a more widely spaced dotted line and, though it may mar sheers, it is useful for marking heavier fabrics.

Nonpermanent Ink Markers

These are felt-tip pens that have either evaporating or water-soluble ink. The evaporating variety can be used on either the wrong or right side of the fabric; it evaporates in less than forty-eight hours. Water-soluble ink disappears when treated with water; test on a swatch for complete removal before using on the right side of fabric.

Quilter's Masking Tape

Use this narrow tape as a seam allowance guide or to hold two pieces of fabric together until they can be sewn. The tape is easily removable and leaves no residue unless left on the fabric for more than eight hours.

FOR CUTTING

Cutting blades should be strong and sharp. Maintain your cutting blades by having them regularly ground/sharpened by a professional; don't use fabric shears to cut other materials.

Shears

Handles curved or bent at an angle allow shears to lie flat and glide on the cutting surface while cutting the fabric. An assortment of shears with blade lengths from 6" to 8" is useful for cutting different weights of fabric and trimming seams. Use inexpensive shears to cut paper.

Sewing Scissors

Scissors have straight, rather than angled, handles, so they won't glide along the cutting table. Use scissors with small short blades for clipping and trimming seams and threads.

Pinking Shears

Heavy-bladed shears with a serrated edge that are useful for trimming the raw edges of ravel-prone fabrics.

Seam Ripper

To avoid snipping your fabirc, use this handy device instead of scissors to rip out incorrect seams. Slip the point under a single stitch and slide the blade to cut the thread.

Weights

Use weights to secure pattern pieces on the fabric while you are cutting. Made of metal, and often shaped like flat discs with a hole in the center, they can be purchased in fabric and craft stores.

Rotary Cutter, Cutting Mat, and Heavy Plastic Rulers

This cutting system is used extensively by quilters and makes short work of cutting straight-sided pieces—especially narrow lengths such as ties or bias strips. However, the size of your cutting mat determines the longest cut you can make, so the system is sometimes impractical.

✄ The rotary cutter looks a lot like a pizza cutter. It has a circular blade that snaps in and out of a plastic handle; the blade can be smooth-edged or pinked-edged. Rotary cutters can give nasty cuts, so buy one with a retractable blade or protective shield, and keep it away from children.

✄ Cutting mats are made of a special plastic that is self-healing. They come in many sizes and colors, but all have 1" grids printed on the surface as guides for straight line cutting. Some mats have printed diagonal lines in addition to the grid.

✄ Heavy transparent gridded rulers serve as measuring and cutting guides.

Using the rotary cutter: Rotary cutting is unlike cutting with shears because you always cut pieces from the left- rather than the right-hand edge of your fabric. If you are new to rotary cutting, make a few sample cuts to see how it works. If you are left-handed, reverse the following directions.

1 First mark a straight edge on your fabric. Place the mat on your table, then place the fabric, marked side up, on the mat. Place the ruler on your fabric, aligned with and to the left of the marked line. Hold the ruler firmly in place with your left hand; hold the cutter with your right hand. Place the blade against the edge of the ruler and apply pressure as you roll the blade away from you to cut along the marked line. Lift the ruler and discard the excess fabric.

2 Once you have cut a straight edge, you won't have to mark any other cutting lines. Align the cut edge of the fabric with a straight line on the cutting mat; the fabric should extend to your right. Align the appropriate guideline on the ruler with the cut edge of the fabric. (For instance, to cut a 2"-wide strip, align the line 2" from the edge of the ruler with the cut edge of the fabric—a 2" width of the ruler should overlap the fabric.) Cut along the edge of the ruler as you did in step 1. Lift the ruler, remove the cut width of fabric, and repeat as necessary. ▽

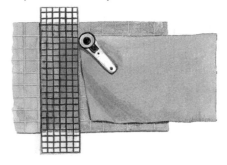

TIPS FROM THE PROS

✄ To cut a piece that is wider than your ruler, first mark the cutting lines on your fabric, then follow step 1 above; reposition the fabric as necessary.

essential equipment

FOR SEWING

You won't need any unusual equipment for sewing most pillows, but the heavier your fabric, the sturdier your machine, thread, and pins should be.

Pins

While you can use standard dressmaker's (stainless steel) pins for home decorating projects, the following are often better alternatives when working with bulkier and heavier decorator fabrics:

✂ Quilting Pins: 1¹/₄" long with large round heads at the top, they look like long dressmaker's pins.

✂ T-Pins: Longer yet than quilting pins, the blunt end of this pin is folded perpendicular to the shaft, making a T shape. Useful when working with bulky and heavy fabrics, and when anchoring fabric to a padded surface.

✂ Glass Head Pins: Fine and super-sharp pins with small glass heads (won't melt with heat while pressing) for sheer and lightweight fabrics.

Adhesives, Interfacings, and Stabilizers

There are a number of products available that help to control fabric, give it body, or hold it together. Some are used to facilitate the sewing process, while others give permanent support.

✂ Interfacings: These woven or nonwoven fabrics are used to reinforce stress points and lend support to fragile fabrics. They are fused or basted to the fabric and the two layers are then treated as one. Back button and buttonhole areas with interfacing; place it in hems if your fabric is soft or sheer. If you are not familiar with the various types, ask your fabric vendor for assistance.

✂ Fusible Webs: These look like lightweight nonwoven interfacing, but they are really sheets of glue. Place them between two pieces of fabric and press to adhere. They tend to add stiffness, but can be useful for small areas. Some webs come in strips that are suitable for hems. Fusible webs are generally permanent.

✂ Sprays: There are permanent and temporary spray adhesives available in both art supply and sewing stores. They are particularly useful if you are layering batting with another fabric, as they save a lot of pinning and ensure a smooth surface. Spray them lightly onto the back of one fabric and then adhere it to another. Test the various products (follow the manufacturer's instructions) to be sure you like the way they work on your fabric.

✂ Stabilizers: There is a whole world of temporary stabilizers, which are used to lend body to fabric during embroidery or quilting, thus preventing puckering. They either wash off, tear away, or brush off.

Threads

Pick the thread that matches the job. When in doubt about color, choose a shade that is slightly darker than the background of your fabric.

✂ All-Purpose Thread: 100% polyester or cotton-covered polyester, this thread is suitable for most projects.

✂ Hand-Basting Thread: Loosely twisted white (only) cotton thread for hand basting fabric pieces; breaks easily.

✂ Upholstery Thread: 100% nylon or 100% polyester, extra strong for sewing heavyweight fabrics. Since it's treated to resist chemicals, rot, and mildew, it's an excellent choice for outdoor items.

✂ Woolly Nylon Thread: Texturized overlock thread that is soft and strong, with ability to stretch and recover. Used primarily for serger rolled hems.

✂ Button, Carpet, Heavy-Duty, and Craft Threads: Strong, heavy, cotton-covered polyester, designed specifically for hand sewing. Use to attach buttons to pillows and cushions.

Hand-Sewing Needles

There are several types of hand-sewing needles, each designed for a specific task. Most types come in different sizes, the higher the number, the thinner the needle. Here are some you'll find useful.

✂ Sharps: Short needles good for general sewing.

✂ Milliner's: Long, flexible needles good for basting or sewing on trim.

✂ Embroidery/Crewel: Large-eyed needles with sharp points.

✂ Tapestry: Large-eyed needles with blunt points.

✂ Upholsterer's/Sailmaker's Assortment: Large, long, sturdy curved and straight needles. Use a curved needle to sew a cover closed on a large pillow form. Use a long needle to tuft (indent) a pillow form or sew buttons through one.

Beeswax

To keep your thread from tangling or knotting when you are sewing by hand, pass it over the surface of a cake of beeswax. Beeswax also controls static electricity in synthetic threads.

TIPS FROM THE PROS

✂ To augment the effect of beeswax, press the strand of waxed thread with a hot iron.

Sewing Machine

Nearly every part of a home decorating project can be sewn on any standard, modern home sewing machine—including buttons, unless they have shank backs. Be sure to use the proper needle size and type for your fabric—consult your owner's manual if unsure.

Serger

A time-saving machine that stitches, trims, and overcasts a seam, performing all three operations simultaneously and at twice the speed of a conventional home sewing machine. If you are not familiar with sergers, test one before purchasing—and be aware that pins must be removed from seams before reaching the needle and knife. Sergers can also create a narrow rolled hem and an edge finish that consists of small, tight stitches and no visible hem allowance, such as those on commercially made napkins.

Embroidery Machine

Embroidery machines have the ability to stitch larger motifs, such as monograms and multicolored patterns, in unlimited varieties. You can use one to create a custom, decorative trim wherever you wish. Some machines can be attached to a personal computer and scanner to customize designs. Some manufacturers supply sewing machines that have built-in embroidery mechanisms, while others have a separate embroidery unit. Many home sewing machines are equipped with some embroidery stitches.

Sewing Machine Feet

Aside from a zipper foot, your regular straight sewing foot is all you really need for any home decorating project. However, some of the following special feet can make certain jobs easier. If you are unfamiliar with them, refer to your owner's manual.

✂Gathering Foot: This foot draws up the fabric to lock fullness into each stitch. It's great for gathering long ruffles or lace trims quickly and evenly.

✂Ruffler Attachment: A large accessory designed to ruffle the edge of fabric in even increments. The density of the gathering can be adjusted.

✂Hemming Foot: A handy device that automatically rolls the fabric into a narrow hem. It is usually available in at least two widths. Hemming feet can be tricky to use, especially on bias edges, so test on a swatch of your fabric.

TIPS FROM THE PROS

✂If you have trouble getting good results with a hemming foot when your machine is set to straight stitch, try it with a zigzag stitch. Be sure the resulting effect is right for your project before using.

✂Quilting Foot: This foot has short, open toes to help you see and stitch along any lines marked on the fabric.

✂Zipper Foot: A narrow presser foot that sits on one side of the needle only. A zipper foot is essential for inserting zippers and for covering and applying welting. If you are using welting, you'll need an adjustable zipper foot—one that can be positioned on either side of the needle—or a pair of fixed feet.

✂Welting/Piping Foot: A presser foot with a cut-out groove on the underside that rides over cording, guiding it evenly and consistently past the needle. This foot is a real time-saver when making or sewing on medium-size welting/piping. The needle can be positioned to the left or right of the cord and shifted so the stitches are closer to it.

✂Leather Roller Foot: This foot is actually a large metal wheel that revolves against the feed and moves the fabric under the needle. It enables you to stitch close to bulky trims.

✂Edgestitch Foot: The upright flange of this foot rides along the edge of a fold or seamline, acting as a guide for straight edgestitching. Adjust the machine needle to the desired distance from the edge and sew, guiding the edge under the flange.

✂Blind Hem Foot: Designed for use with a special zigzag stitch, this foot guides the fabric and enables you to quickly produce a nearly invisible hem.

✂Button Foot: This foot enables you to sew on buttons with a zigzag stitch; it automatically creates the proper thread tension. To keep the fabric from advancing under the needle when using a button foot, drop the machine feed.

✂Buttonhole Foot: Designed to be used with the automatic buttonhole settings on the machine, this foot is calibrated with a buttonhole length guide and grooved to hold the fabric taut as it rides over the stitches.

✂Foot-Lifter for Bulky Intersections: This small device is not a foot, but enables your presser foot to ride smoothly over bulky intersecting seams. Slip it under the foot as needed and remove it when you've stitched across the seam.

essential equipment

FOR PRESSING

All you really need for pressing a pillow project is a decent iron and an ironing board. However, there are many other pressing aids; the various blocks and small boards not only help with specific pressing tasks, they can be slipped inside a pillow cover to support a small area, enabling you to press without creasing other portions of the cover.

Iron

A standard steam/dry iron is fine for all projects. If using the steam setting, be sure your iron does not spit, and fill it with distilled water as a precaution against stains. Place a pressing cloth between the iron and the fabric, or press on the wrong side of the fabric.

Steam Press

This commercial-type press is made in various models for the home sewer; it presses large areas efficiently. It is also good for fusing large amounts of fusible interfacings.

Pressing Cloth

To prevent scorch and shine, place a cloth between the iron and fabric. Commercial pressing cloths are available in fabric stores, but a piece of muslin, batiste, or a tea towel (not terry cloth) works too.

Padded Surface

Press seams, tucks, pleats, darts, hems, etc., on a flat, stable, padded surface, such as an ironing board or a table or other surface that is protected with a thick felt pad, wool blanket, cotton batting, or commercially prepared ironing board pad.

TIPS FROM THE PROS

✁Cover the padded pressing surface with heavy cotton fabric, such as drill (an undyed twill weave similar to denim). Teflon-treated covers are nonabsorbent and repel steam, so the fabric being pressed on them tends to lift or shift position.

Seam Roll

Press long seams, zipper applications, and narrow areas over this densely stuffed, fabric-covered roll, which is about 2" in diameter.

Hams

Mold and shape darts, curved and shaped seams, and hard-to-reach places by pressing them over a ham. Available in several shapes and sizes, these fabric-covered forms are either filled with finely processed sawdust or are molded in polyurethane.

Clapper

To flatten bulky seams, facings, creases, pleats, and points, place them on the pressing surface and pound gently with a clapper, made of a smooth high-quality hardwood.

Point Presser

Slide the pointed end of this narrow, shaped hardwood block inside corners, points, and other hard-to-reach places.

Sleeve Board

Use this double-sided small ironing board when pressing narrow, hard-to-reach places. Most sleeve boards collapse for storage.

Pile-Surfaced Boards

To avoid crushing pile or napped fabrics, press them face down on one of several types of pile-surfaced boards. The most traditional is a needle board, which is a specially constructed bed of steel needles set upright in a fabric pad. There are newer varieties, one of which resembles a field of hook-and-loop fastener hooks. Purchase the largest board you can afford so that you can press the largest possible area at one time.

TIPS FROM THE PROS

✁When using a needle board, avoid pressing along the edge of the needle bed—it will leave a permanent mark on most pile fabrics.

Bias Binding Maker

When strips of bias fabric are fed through this handy device they emerge with both long edges folded to the center, so they are easy to press into binding or ties. Bias binding makers are available in sizes that produce $1/2$"-, $3/4$"-, 1"-, and 2"-wide folded tapes.

index

acknowledgments

PHOTOGRAPHY ACKNOWLEDGMENTS

Part One: 8–9: George Ross; stylist: Karin Strom. **10:** Tria Giovan. **11:** Andrew McKinney; design: Laura Ashley/Tres McKinney. **12:** Tria Giovan. **13:** Richard Mandelkorn; design: Karen O'Brien, Bloomingdale's Design Group. **14:** Bradley Olman. **15:** Tria Giovan. **16:** Andrew McKinney. **17:** Bradley Olman. **18:** Andrew McKinney; design: Laura Ashley/Tres McKinney. **19:** Maryann Kressig; photographed at Corner George Inn, Maeystown, Illinois. **All fabric baskets:** Michael Chan; fabrics courtesy of Waverly. **Part Two: All photographs:** George Ross; stylist: Karin Strom. **Part Three: 106–107:** Michael Chan; fabrics courtesy of Waverly.

PROJECT ACKNOWLEDGMENTS

The pillow samples were made by Linda Lee Design Associates, Topeka, Kansas, with help from Stephanie Valley, Darchelle Woltkamp, Dort Johnson, Bernie Holsteen, Kathy Davis, Marge Cole, Sharon Ruddy.

The editors would like to thank the following for assistance with materials for the samples: B. Berger; Calico Corners; Duralee Fabrics; F. Schumacher & Co.; Fairmont Fabrics; H. Lynn White; Kravet Fabrics, Inc.; Norbar Fabrics; Payne Fabrics; Robert Allen; Stroheim & Romann, Inc.; Threadwear, Topeka, Kansas; Waverly; Westgate Fabrics.